A Treasure Hunting Text

Ram Publications
Hal Dawson, Editor

Treasure Hunting for Fun and Profit
Exciting tales of discoveries illustrate Charles Garrett's careful explanation of how he finds treasure with a modern metal detector.

Ghost Town Treasures: Ruins, Relics and Riches
Step-by-step explanations on how to search ghost towns and deserted structures; which detectors to use and methods for using them.

The New Successful Coin Hunting
The world's most authoritative guide to finding valuable coins, totally rewritten to include instructions for 21st Century detectors.

Modern Metal Detectors
Comprehensive guide to metal detectors; designed to increase understanding and expertise about all aspects of these electronic marvels.

Treasure Recovery from Sand and Sea
Easy-to-follow instructions for reaching the "blanket of wealth" beneath sands nearby and under the world's waters; rewritten for the 90's.

Gold Panning is Easy
Excellent field guide shows the beginner exactly how to find and pan gold; follow these instructions and perform as well as any professional.

You Can Find Gold with a Metal Detector
Explains in layman's terms how to use a modern detector to find gold nuggets and veins; includes instructions for panning and dredging.

Buried Treasures You Can Find
Complete field guide for finding treasure; includes state-by-state listing of thousands of sites where treasure is believed to exist.

Sunken Treasure: How to Find It
One of the world's foremost underwater salvors shares a lifetime's experience in locating and recovering treasure from deep beneath the sea.

Gold of the Americas
A history of the precious metal and how it helped shape the history of the Americas; filled with colorful vignettes and stories of bravery and greed.

The Competitive Treasure Hunt
How to plan, organize and win a treasure hunt; all you need to know about the fascinating world of competitive treasure hunting.

You Can Find GOLD

RAM
BOOKS

With a Metal Detector

Charles Garrett ✦ Roy Lagal

ISBN 0-915920-86-7
Library of Congress Catalog Card No. 95-74805
You CAN Find Gold...with a Metal Detector
Copyright 1995
Charles Garrett
Ram Publishing Company

Fourteenth Printing, June 2010

Book and cover design by Mel Climer
Back cover photo by Hal Dawson

For FREE listing of treasure hunting books write

Ram Publishing Company
P.O. Box 38649   •   Dallas, TX 75238

You CAN Find Gold...

Contents

With a Metal Detector

By Charles Garrett

Treasure Hunting Texts

Ghost Town Treasures: Ruins, Relics and Riches
Real Gold in Those Golden Years
Let's Talk Treasure Hunting
Treasure Recovery from Sand and Sea
Successful Coin Hunting
Modern Metal Detectors
Treasure Hunting Pays Off
Treasure Hunting Secrets

True Treasure Tales

The Secret of John Murrell's Vault
The Missing Nez Perce Gold

By Roy Lagal

Gold Panning is Easy
Weekend Prospecting
Find an Ounce of Gold a Day

By Garrett and Lagel

Modern Treasure Hunting
Modern Electronic Prospecting

Charles Garrett
Roy Lagal

harles Garrett and Roy Lagal keenly feel the lure of gold. They love to hunt for it with a metal detector. They understand why others want to hunt. Finding a massive nugget is a fond dream for both, but they are satisfied with the joy of a small one or even just a little color in their pans. Furthermore, Charles sympathizes with nearly every other metal detector enthusiast like himself who would *rather* be using the instrument to hunt for gold — whether he or she admits it or not.

On the other hand, Roy has spent a lifetime as a professional prospector. His success in finding gold literally determined if (or how well) he and his late wife Gerri would eat!

Both men are ready to share their lifetimes of experience to help hobbyists get started (or, improve) their performance in the gold fields.

And, what a lifetime it has been for both!

Charles Garrett

Charles Garrett certainly did not set out to become a leading manufacturer of metal detection equipment. He prepared himself well, however, to become one of the world's foremost treasure hunters. Since boyhood he has been enthralled with stories of hidden wealth...tales which brought excitement to his semi-rural youth in the Piney Woods of Deep East Texas. Throughout his life he has continually sought to learn more about techniques and equipment for treasure hunting and finding gold.

Today, the name of Charles Garrett ranks high on any list of those men and women who have pioneered the development and use of metal detectors...whether for discovery of gold or treasure hunting...for security...or, for any other reason.

As a young electrical engineering graduate of Lamar University and veteran of Navy service during the Korean conflict, Charles was deeply engrossed in development of systems and equipment required by America's fledgling space effort in the early 1960s. Also devoting himself to his lifetime hobby of treasure hunting, however, he designed and built metal detectors in his spare time.

Because of the versatility and performance of his detectors, they became popular with fellow treasure hunters for whom he was soon making them. This avocation became a career when he founded Garrett Electronics to produce his inventions.

Charles has become recognized as an unofficial spokesman for the hobby of treasure hunting and the metal detecting industry. His complete biography includes a long list of honors, personal appearances and books. He is the author of several major works which have been accepted as veritable "texts" for metal detecting. He and Roy coined the term "electronic prospecting."

His Company is also the world's foremost manufacturer of security metal detection equipment. Not only do its famed Magnascanner and Super Scanner instruments protect air travelers all over the world, but they have been honored as the choice to safeguard historical and cultural treasures, Olympic athletes, presidents and kings.

He is married to the former Eleanor Smith of Pennington, Texas, who has played a key role in the growth of Garrett Electronics. They have two sons and a daughter.

As a graduate engineer and a businessman, Charles introduced discipline to the manufacture of metal detection equipment. He has generally raised the standards of using these instruments everywhere, while the hobby itself has grown from a haphazard pastime to almost a science.

Garrett quality is known throughout the world. From the beginning, Charles Garrett vowed "to practice what I preach" — in other words, to test his equipment in the field...to insure that it will work for customers, regardless of ground conditions and environment. Thus, with a metal detector of his own design he has searched for and found treasure on every continent except Antarctica. He has also scanned under lakes, seas and oceans of the world.

Roy Lagal

The biography of Roy Lagal truly describes a treasure hunting legend: boyhood on the Kansas-Oklahoma border amid tales of settler's caches and the hidden wealth of Osage and Cherokee Indians...Army service with mine detectors during World War II...more than a quarter-century actively pursuing great treasures of America's last frontier.

Roy smiles as he reminisces about the time he and his bride Gerri set out for full-time treasure hunting half a century ago. "We aimed for a big 'un," he recalls, "the Lost Dutchman mine in Arizona, and we went broke before we found it."

This genial and modest man wouldn't mind if you believed "going broke before we found it" the story of his life, but long-time treasure hunters can assure you otherwise. For nearly 30 years Roy and Gerri traveled over the West — and, even to Florida — as they hunted for gold, caches and other treasures. They often lived in the ghost

3

towns they explored and beside the mountain streams where they were panning. Home was where their hats were. Yet, these decades of rambling were also punctuated by achievements such as patenting the Gravity Trap® gold pan, helping Charles Garrett develop the Scorpion Gold Stinger™ metal detector and writing classic texts on metal detecting and gold panning. Too, after settling in Nez Perce Indian country, Roy became recognized as one of the world's experts in their lore and the recovery of Indian caches.

How he loves to talk of caches...those that might have been found and all those he continues to research and seek! Still, like other great treasure hunters, he's silent about his own recoveries. "I've panned a little gold, detected some and found a few caches," he'll grudgingly admit, "but probably no more than one a year when it's all figgered out" Yet, that "one a year" plus his work with metal detectors, gold pans and writing "figgers out" Roy to be a contented and successful man indeed.

This book is the invitation to hobbyists by Charles and Roy to join them *in the field* as they search for gold in all its forms.

Hal Dawson
Editor, Ram

Dallas, Texas
Autumn 1995

4

Hunting for Gold
Something We Love...

This book is designed to explain clearly the steps necessary for finding gold with a metal detector. It is written in simple, layman's language. Whether you have never used a metal detector or have years of successful experience with them, you will know more about hunting for gold after you read and study this book.

For, that's what it's all about...finding gold! We're not going to be talking about coins, jewelry, relics or any other popular detector targets. This book is entirely about gold-hunting.

And, believe us, hunting for gold is different! No matter how much success you've had in the park, on the beach or anywhere else in using a metal detector...no matter how many coins, relics or gold rings you've found, you'll need to acquaint yourself with different techniques to maximize your success in the gold fields. Yes, you *can* be successful. We urge you never to doubt yourself. Take our word for it. If you're using a modern detector in the proper manner and if you persevere, you *will* find gold!

For almost two decades the guidebook for seeking gold and other precious metals with a detector was one called *Electronic Prospecting*, which we wrote. Prospectors in the field recognized it as a book written exclusively for them. We knew our subject well and the instructions we offered in it had been proven by our field experience. We believe our expertise was evident.

We two coined the phrase "electronic prospecting," which almost sounds a little too high and mighty today. What we want to talk about in this book is simply "finding gold" with a metal detector.

In this new book we will again be calling on our experiences over a lifetime. Between us we know how a prospector thinks and what he is looking for. Yet, we also understand how a metal detector can help both amateurs and professionals find gold.

And, it is true that our *Electronic Prospecting* was an instant success and remained successful. It underwent continual reprintings and its text was regularly updated. Recent developments, however, particularly in computerized metal detectors, have radically changed the metal detector as we know it. Today's instrument is a far cry from those in use even a decade ago. And, the results of all these improvements are being demonstrated daily in the field. Finding gold is so much easier now with a modern metal detector than ever before.

This new book will tell you how to find gold, whether you call it "electronic prospecting" or whatever else you please. Those of you who loved the original book and have come to memorize passages from it will occasionally encounter familiar ground here. The laws of physics and the lore of prospecting have not changed. Yet, you will also find much in this book that is new, particularly regarding the use and application of recently developed gold-hunting equipment. As its title indicates, the book is designed to prove to you that *You CAN Find Gold...With a Metal Detector.* This book is, indeed, written for the prospectors of the 21st century who are eager to make their job easier by using the most modern electronic metal detecting equipment available. If you encounter terms you don't understand, refer to the Glossary.

We find tremendous enjoyment in going out into God's great outdoors to search for gold. The times when we're able to do this (and, they are not nearly often enough) come as close to "heaven on earth" as we've ever found.

We wish that everyone could share our joy. So, whether you'll be just a "weekend prospector" or plan to get really serious about searching for gold, we sincerely believe that this book will help you. And, if it takes you outdoors into the gold fields, we'll be especially happy. For, some day when we're out searching for nuggets we hope to...

See you in the field!

Charles Garrett   Roy Lagal

Garland, Texas
Clarkston, Idaho
Autumn 1995

Chapter 1

Gold

Its Lure and Lore...

Rich as Croesus...the Midas touch...Jason and the Golden Fleece...El Dorado...the history, folklore and mythology of mankind is filled with references to the precious metal. Gold has been revered since the dawn of time.

The ancients considered it the metal of the sun, and like the sun it could not be destroyed or even damaged. Fire and heat turned metals of lesser value into waste matter. Gold merely softened, then dissolved into a liquid until heat was removed, allowing it to return to its hardened state. Because of these properties gold was one of the first metals ever "worked" by primitive man.

Prized as an ornament, a symbol of wealth, a means of barter, the yellow metal has played a vital role in world history. Kingdoms were won and lost because of gold. New lands were sought out and conquered. The value of gold and the quest for it helped draw the map of the entire Western Hemisphere and explains why Spanish is spoken almost exclusively between the Rio Grande and the Antarctic while the natural resources of most of North America accrued to English-speaking peoples.

It is not known when gold was first discovered, but gold cups and jewelry made as early as 3500 B.C. have been dug at Ur in Mesopotamia. The skilled craftsmanship shown in these gold objects suggests that the craft of working gold had been developed centuries prior to the date attributed to these particular excavated objects. The story of the ancient world was indeed written in gold. Even when it was too scarce for daily transactions, the precious metal was a symbol of wealth for ancient civilizations — in China from about 1200 B.C.; Egypt, 1000 B.C.; and in Babylon and Minoa from the third century B.C.

Then in the 16th century the quest for gold resulted directly in the greatest conquest of new lands that will ever be seen in the history of our world as the Spanish plundered ancient civilizations throughout the Americas to enrich the royal storehouses of Madrid. There was four times as much gold and silver in circulation in 1600 than when Columbus first landed in the New World just a little more than a century before.

Throughout the latter half of the 19th century the search for gold and other precious metals hastened the development of the new United States of America and played a significant role in both its boundary lines and its

Over

By identifying a sample as metal or mineral a detector leaves no doubt about whether this discovery is a valuable piece of ore or a worthless rock.

Facing

Charles Garrett displays a handsome nugget he detected while searching a remote and rugged abandoned ore road on a mountain in Utah.

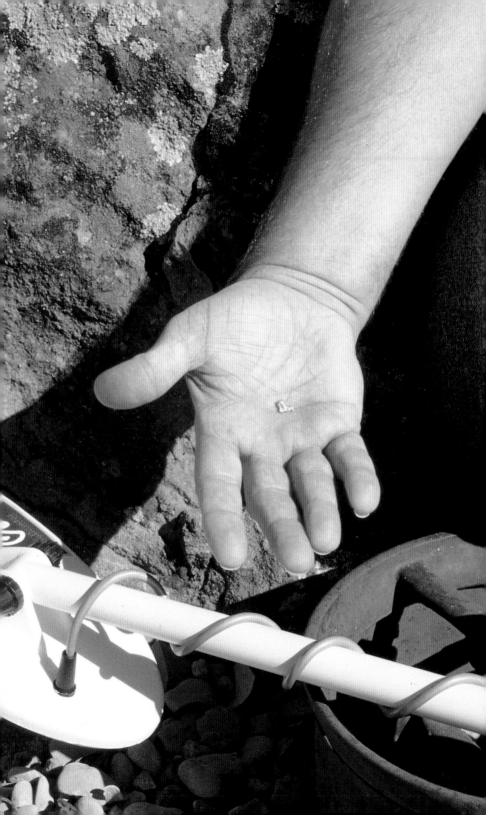

destiny. Nine days before a peace treaty with Mexico would officially bring the California territory into the United States...on January 24, 1848, at a place now called Coloma on the South Fork of the American River, about 35 miles northeast of Sacramento...John Marshall, a carpenter from New Jersey, picked up gold nuggets from the stream where Captain John Sutter was constructing a sawmill. And, the first great United States gold rush had begun.

The world was in trouble in 1848...the Potato Famine in Ireland, grinding poverty in England, tumult across the post-Napoleonic Continent with iron military rule in Germany, Unrest was everywhere. The news from the Pacific Coast of the New World brought hope that life could be better. Thousands of Europeans set sail for America. Many went around Cape Horn, directly to California.

In the United States times had not been good since the Panic of 1837. The question of slavery was slowing expansion. An ambitious young man without funds had

Over

A major benefit of searching for gold with a metal detector is the beautiful outdoor scenery to which the pastime will often lead a hobbyist.

Facing

The elliptical Crossfire searchcoil helped a hobbyist to discover this beautiful nugget in a pile of rocks; a plastic gold pan pan was then used in its recovery.

little to look forward to...until he heard tales of the fortunes being found, literally, on the ground in California. Every river that flowed out of the high Sierras seemed to carry gold with it. The Feather and the Yuba to the north, the Mokelumne and Stanislaus to the south, were just as rich as the American.

San Francisco grew from a tiny seaport to a city of 25,000 in a year's time. So many prospectors went to California that the territory had enough people to be admitted as a state in 1850.

The influx of prospectors who came first to California during the early years of its Gold Rush and later moved on to Colorado, Nevada, Montana, South Dakota and other areas hastened the development of the western United States. The gold of the West, for example, paid for the first railroad across the nation. The railroad was built by four 49'ers who had come west to search for gold but found it easier to sell dry goods, groceries and miners' tools. They were Charles Crocker, Mark Hopkins, Colis P. Huntington and Leland Stanford.

Hard on the heels of the California gold rush came another one around the world. When Edward Hargraves, English by birth, panned for gold in California's Stanislaus River, he recognized country similar to that of Australia where he had grown up. So, he went back to the land "down under" and discovered gold in New South Wales in 1851 to begin another mad scramble with gold as the prize. California and Australia between them, then, produced almost as much gold in the next 10 years as the entire world had ever dug before.

The search for gold continues to this day. Countless tons of gold have been taken from the earth by professional miners, using expensive equipment and sophisticated methods. Cursory study of geography, geology and chemistry reveals, however, that most of the gold on Earth is still waiting to be recovered. In 1849 world production was 11,866 ounces and climbed dramatically, reaching a peak of 2,782,018 ounces in 1856. Nine years later production had declined below a million ounces. The great California Gold Rush was over. Miners and prospectors had moved on to the greener — and more golden — pastures.

Between 1792 and 1933 the United States Mint struck off more than $4.5 billion in gold coins. The first mint at Philadelphia made $10 eagles, half-eagles and quarter-eagles. Most of the gold came from Spanish and French traders in the Southwest. In 1838 mints were opened in Charlotte, North Carolina, and Dahlonega, Georgia, near new gold fields. Gold money was scarce until the California discovery in 1848. With the flood of California gold two new coins were minted, a gold dollar and a double eagle worth $20. Because it took so long for California gold to travel across the country, private companies there issued their own gold coins which are highly valued by collectors today. In 1854 the San Francisco mint opened to handle the coinage of California gold.

Incidentally, do you know why gold coins have a reddish hue? It's because they contain one part copper to nine parts gold — to harden them!

Even with surface gold removed from the Mother Lode country of California, numerous geological surveys and studies have suggested that only some 15 to 20% of the gold in California has actually been recovered. Based on this data, it seems obvious that a vast amount of gold still remains to be discovered...not only in California, but in all other parts of the world.

You believe that gold is not present in the area where you live? Perhaps no one has looked hard enough for it!

20th Century Gold Rush

Gold was a medium of exchange in the United States until 1933 when new legislation made it illegal for citizens to own gold other than coins, jewelry, nuggets and the like in collections. This ban was among the measures inaugurated by President Franklin D. Roosevelt in the early days of his presidency as he sought to shore up the economy of the nation at the depths of the Great Depression.

During more than four decades after private ownership of bullion was prohibited, the U.S. government arbitrarily maintained the international value of gold at $35 per ounce. As recovery from World War II led to worldwide economic expansion during the 50s and 60s this price became unrealistically low, especially by 1974 standards when the ban on ownership was ended and a free market was allowed to determine gold prices.

Of course, the price of gold immediately soared. In the harrowing times of steep inflation and high interest that followed, this price sometimes exceeded $800 per ounce. Such a sharp gain in value, coupled with man's adventurous spirit, caused a small-scale gold rush back to the 19th-century camps and ghost towns of the American West. Metal detector manufacturers benefited commensurately. With the Garrett factory in full production during the boom, detector deliveries lagged some three months behind sales.

Although the price of gold has decreased significantly from its highs of the early 1980's, it remains — as this book is written — some 11 times greater than it was when the ban on ownership was lifted in 1974. Furthermore, there is no doubt that a strong demand for gold exists in the private sector. With its industrial use steadily increasing, prices can be expected to rise generally — especially in relation to international economic conditions.

Who is Prospecting?

Doctors, attorneys, businessmen, students, senior citizens...entire families...from all walks of life and all income levels have found that the healthful, relaxed outdoor life of weekend or vacation prospecting can yield dividends — in dollars and cents as well as pure pleasure. A single ounce of gold for many is worth the equivalent of several days' pay. One fair-sized nugget's value can exceed a month's salary. These "instant riches" are obviously part of the attraction of the business/hobby known as recreational mining or weekend prospecting.

Just as the 19th-century prospectors sought to control their own fate and fortune through the discovery of nature's wealth, so do many of today's seekers after gold. The spirit of the 49'ers and of the Klondike prevails among both professional and recreational prospectors who have discovered the pleasures and profits of searching for gold.

Men and women, boys and girls who are seeking gold work at regular jobs, but on weekends, holidays and vacations they join families and friends to head for one of the many thousands of areas open to the public where gold can be found. They set up camp by a stream, then use pan or dredge along with their metal detector to find gold. Or, they may travel to an old ghost town or deserted mining camp and scan for nuggets, ore veins or valuable mineral/ore specimens overlooked by early day prospectors who operated without the benefit of electronic equipment.

Modern Equipment

Three developments have greatly increased the ability of the recreational miner to hit paydirt in comparison with the sourdough prospectors who flooded California in the 1850s and went to Alaska at the turn of the century:

1. Availability of easy-to-use, highly efficient gold pans and portable sluices;

2. Production of lightweight, portable dredges that can be effectively operated by one or two people;

3. Development of the metal detector. This single tool makes locating precious metals simpler for *all* prospectors, no matter what their level of experience, no matter where they are searching...on land or in the water. And this tool is immeasurably better today than it was even a decade ago.

After World War II army veterans who had encountered mine detectors during their military service (such as Roy Lagal) recognized the potential of these devices for finding precious metals. Professional prospectors were also quick to adapt themselves to their use.

Simply stated, metal detectors could and did find gold. Searching for precious metals was, thus, a primary purpose of both the war surplus instruments and the first metal detectors manufactured commercially in the years following the war. And, the early BFO detectors, rudimentary as they were, represented a distinct improvement over the military mine detectors and were successful in finding gold. By the late 70s detectors had continued to improve, and these newly developed instruments enjoyed varying degrees of greater success, depending on the expertise and determination of the individuals using them. These rugged yet quite sensitive ground-canceling instruments were capable of operating in difficult, even highly mineralized, terrain.

Today's computerized instruments are another story entirely. As discussed in Chapters Six and Seven, these detectors are products essentially of the past half dozen years. The detectors that are available today being used by prospectors who will be seeking gold in the 21st century represent an even greater improvement over the detectors of ten years ago than did those 1985 instruments over the war-surplus mine detectors we used in the late 40s.

That's right! Today's metal detectors, discussed in this book, present a gold-finding tool such as that never possessed before by any prospector. These relatively inexpensive detectors are amazingly simple to use and have already proven themselves to be effective goldfinders. Yes, it's easy to find gold with a modern metal detector.

Read on to learn how!

Chapter 2

Where

To Look for Gold...

Gold can be found in nature throughout the United States — in all 50 states — and just about everywhere else, for that matter. Although these are true statements, they are more than a little misleading. Traces of the precious yellow metal may be *physically present* just about everywhere, but *sufficient quantities* to make prospecting possible, much less profitable, occur rarely — in only about half of the states, for example. In the others gold is either so fine or in such minute quantities that its presence is a fact of chemistry rather than of potential wealth. Recovery is not only impractical here but virtually impossible...especially for the recreational prospector.

Contrary to prevailing opinion, gold has been produced in quantity in states other than those concentrated in the Rocky Mountains or west of them. In fact, gold was first discovered and mined in the United States in North Carolina in 1799. Georgia had the first gold rush in America in 1828, although it could scarcely compare with the California rush two decades later. Of course, there were discoveries made by Native Americans and Spanish explorers in the Southwest and Far West before the advent of Europeans into these areas.

States where gold can be found and recovered effectively are located from ocean to ocean and from border to border. The major gold production states, listed roughly in their order of total production:

California	Arizona	South Carolina
Colorado	Oregon	Tennessee
South Dakota	Idaho	Virginia
Alaska	Washington	Alabama
Nevada	New Mexico	Texas
Utah	North Carolina	Michigan
Montana	Wyoming	Wisconsin
	Georgia	

Production from these states has amounted to more than 300 million ounces — or well over a trillion dollars at today's price. It is obvious that gold production in the United States has been no "nickle-and-dime" matter, and production continues at this moment in many of the above states.

How can you locate a site to begin your search for gold most successfully?

It's really quite simple. The answer lies in research. Study the list of states and the map on the facing page that shows areas of production. Use the Appendix of this book and the facilities of your public library. Seek out other sources of information.

Locate the areas of production that you can feasibly visit — on vacation or at any other time. Then, after a little research, using all of the sources that you might discover, you can determine a logical *where* for you to begin your search. Complete your research *before* you hasten off to the gold fields. It will pay off for you in the end!

Do Some Investigating

Once you have selected those area(s) in which you wish to prospect, check with the governmental agencies and request information and/or literature that would be of assistance to you. Federally owned lands, located generally in the Western states, are under the supervision of the Bureau of Land Management. Their regional offices

U.S. Gold Locations

which are listed in this book offer valuable information and pamphlets on staking claims and other matters that are important to prospectors. The U.S. Forest Service also supervises vast amounts of land. Their regional headquarters offices for the Western states are also listed.

Most states have some sort of Bureau of Mines or Geological Surveys which can provide information on the incidence of gold in particular areas. They can also be helpful in supplying information on prospecting geology and gold recovery. A listing of the addresses of the Bureaus of Mines in the Western states is included in the Appendix. Seek out the Bureau of Mines or Geology in every state in which you might have an interest. You might be surprised at the information that is available on prospecting for gold with a metal detector.

Still other sources of information are the appropriate state Tourist Bureaus. As the value of tourism has come to be more widely appreciated, some states have prepared maps and other materials showing the locations of gold deposits, gem fields, ghost towns, mining districts and other points that might interest the hobbyist seeking gold with a metal detector. When you write to these tourist bureaus, ask specifically about information on searching for gold.

Since you will probably be interested primarily in nuggets, you'll need to ask yourself several questions. Are there dredge tailing piles to work? Are there good placer areas where you may find nuggets?

Go to public and school libraries. Look for information on the gold districts in which you plan to work. Find out about the prospecting that has already been carried out in this area; it may give you a better indication of your chances. Always try to find out what kind of gold was produced in the areas you intend to investigate. You will be more successful in mining areas where free milling gold was produced than in those where gold production required complicated chemical processing or leaching techniques to recover the metal. Areas where only very fine gold was found do not offer good prospects for finding nuggets with a detector.

On the other hand, you may decide to search for veins of gold ore in old mines or by field searching. Decide *precisely* what type of prospecting you are going to attempt, and then equip yourself accordingly.

If possible, talk to other hobbyists who have worked with metal detectors or gold pans in the mining districts where you intend to explore. There is absolutely no question that your chances of success will increase in proportion to your familiarity with an area. Of course, proper equipment will enable you to be even more effective in your recovery efforts. Know *where* you plan to work before you ever set out for the gold fields, and you will have a far better chance of returning with some good specimens, be they placer, nuggets or ore samples.

Finally, always remember that the chances of a major new discovery are extremely remote since most areas have been searched over the years by literally thousands of prospectors, some who were highly professional and armed with elaborate equipment. Even then, mining experts have estimated that only one prospector out of several thousand ever finds anything worth developing. Moreover, only one out of every three or four hundred properties developed ever becomes a profitable mine.

By concentrating your search in areas that have produced gold in the past, chances for you as a weekend prospector are much greater than if you just wander about aimlessly. It's well to keep in mind the facts of history: any prospector today — amateur or professional — is following in the bootsteps of hundreds — perhaps, thousands — of prospectors and miners who earned their livelihood through finding the precious metal.

Remember that many obvious locations have produced great amounts of gold in the past and continue producing to this day. But, remember also that conditions change, especially over hundreds and thousands of years. Large deposits of gold may have been left by nature in places that look highly unlikely today. Gold is where *you* find it!

Other things that you will find when you search the gold fields thoroughly are old coins — perhaps a cache, if you are lucky — and relics that were left behind by the early prospectors Such items as hand-forged tools make a handsome addition to any hobbyist's collection. So, you may be a winner in the gold fields even if your search does not lead you to large nuggets.

Most importantly, however, we urge you to be enthusiastic and optimistic about your prospects of bringing home a nugget or two or a little dust. Have faith in your abilities and in your detector. Whenever we discuss hunting for gold, we like to recall a casual remark made by a highly successful "amateur" prospector in Utah. He said, "It's easy to find gold, but it's darned near impossible to make a living at it!"

Thus, it behooves us to enjoy gold-finding as a hobby and not to become grandiose or greedy.

Chapter 3

Recovery
Methods of Retrieving Gold...

This is a book about finding gold with a metal detector. As such it will not delve very deeply into the chemistry or physics of the precious metal. But it is important to understand that pure gold is heavy...almost 20 times as heavy as water. And, it is a dense metal. If a ton of pure gold were cast into a cube, no dimension would be much more than 14 inches. The value of this golden block only a little more than 14 inches long, 14 inches wide and 14 inches tall would be something over $100 million, give or take a few hundred thousand dollars, depending up current prices.

Gold is very malleable and ductile. It can be pounded into sheets unbelievably thin. A cubic inch of gold can be hammered into a leaf four-millionth of an inch thick that will cover nearly 1400 square feet. A million of these thin sheets of gold would make a stack only about three inches high. In fact, gold leaf can be pounded so thin that its particles will disappear into the pores of the skin when it is crumbled. One troy ounce (roughly 10% heavier than an avoirdupois ounce) of gold can be drawn into a wire 50 miles long.

Most important to those of us seeking the precious metal with a detector, gold is where you find it! And, you must *find* gold before you can begin to solve the age-old mysteries of recovering it. Some areas naturally are going to produce more "color" than others. You should always remember that as a *heavy* metal gold will tend to follow the shortest path as it moves along in a stream or river. When you study flowing water and find a long stretch where it moves rapidly, be alert for cracks, crevices or other anomalies on the bottom. They may have stopped the movement of the gold in years and centuries gone by and continue to trap it. At the end of such long stretches remember always to search for gold on the *inside* of bends in the river. Since gold will always seek the shortest distance in its downhill path, it will "cut across" wide turns. Check also behind boulders and gravel bars where gold might have settled when the water that was carrying it along slowed down.

To find gold any prospector must first go to where gold exists freely in nature. For the weekend prospector, armed with only a detector and gold pan, the proof of such existence must be historical production of gold in an area. The major gold-bearing regions of the United States and Canada are generally known. In the U.S. they include most of the Western states, a few Southeastern states and Alaska. Ontario, Quebec and British Columbia have been the areas of most activity in Canada.

Although the weekend prospector scarcely needs much knowledge of geology, it helps to understand the nature and characteristics of gold as well as how it originated. Gold is believed to have formed in the depths of the earth millions of years ago. Volcanic activity then released gold and other elements in both gaseous and liquid form, forced upward by tremendous pressures and extreme heat. With its fluid nature gold was forced into cracks, pores and fissures of rocks to form veins or lodes, which have been man's principal source of gold.

Gold is found in lode (vein) deposits, in placer deposits and in sea water. Weekend prospectors are generally seeking gold in placer deposits, which consist of larger particles commonly referred to as nuggets and grains of gold of varying sizes found in streambeds, both wet and dry. These particles have been washed and carried away from a lode, or vein, by surface waters, usually the result of floods.

Over the thousands of centuries that lodes were being broken up and deposited in streams, the entire topography of regions was changing constantly. Massive landslides and upheavals often dammed rivers and created new bodies of water while old streambeds were left dry. Thus, concentrations of placer gold can often be found far from any flowing water because at some time in the distant past a stream *did* flow there. Gold flakes and nuggets remain in a desert after the streams that once irrigated it have been diverted. In fact, if a major new discovery of placer gold were to be made today, it probably would come in some ancient, unmined riverbed. All of the streams that are now flowing have already been well explored.

Placers, then, are created by the weathering of lodes…through the grinding of glaciers and the relentless erosion of wind, rain and snow. In addition, temperatures cause the lode-bearing rocks to contract and expand. Chunks of rock have broken off or eroded away, and earth tremors and rockslides have caused further disruption. Pieces of the lode, ranging in size from flakes to large nuggets, were carried downhill by the normal run-off of rainwater until they reached a stream or river. Thus, placer deposits are the result of decomposition and the wearing away of veins and lodes.

The Gold Pan

Absolutely no experience is required for a beginner to enjoy success in the first panning session. Believe us, this is true!

And, regardless of whether you intend to recover gold by locating it with a metal detector, capturing it in a dredge or by sluicing, a gold pan will remain your *primary tool*. Pans will obviously be necessary in streams, but you will also find them useful far away from water, often in ways that the amateur prospector could never imagine. Dry panning is sometimes the only practical way of discovering gold in desert areas. The pan may also be used for easy recovery of metallic targets signaled by your detector...objects that might be difficult or impossible to locate otherwise.

Simply stated, if you intend to seek gold in the field, it is vital that you not only have a good gold pan but that you understand its importance and know how to use it properly. Of course, we believe the finest and most effective gold pan today to be the **Gravity Trap** pan. Invented by Roy Lagal (U.S. Patent #4,162,969) and manufactured by Garrett Electronics, its effectiveness has been proven by worldwide success and acceptance. Made of unbreakable polypropylene, the pan is far lighter and easier to handle than any metal pan. More importantly, the Gravity Trap pan has built-in gold traps in the form of sharp 90-degree riffles. These riffles are designed to trap the heavier gold and allow fast panning-off of unwanted sand, rocks and gravel.

The pan is forest green in color which has been proved in extensive laboratory and field tests to show gold, garnets, precious gems and black sand better than other colors, including black. After only a little practice, a weekend or recreational placer miner using this new pan can work with equal or greater efficiency than the most proficient professional using an old style metal pan

Placer gold deposits are found in streams such as this one in which Charles Garrett is digging to bedrock for material which he will test by panning.

or one made of black plastic. More information on this pan and its uses can be found in Chapter 5.

Today's recreational miner can achieve excellent results by using a modern metal detector to locate deposits of gold, then panning them with a Gravity Trap gold pan. Whether gold is found in profitable quantities or not, the pleasure of sitting at the edge of mountain stream or in a long-forgotten dry gulch is one that should not be overlooked. Meanwhile the panner is seeking to produce income with two bare hands, knowing full well that the chance always exists of hitting "the big one."

Since all Garrett gold recovery devices can be used for both wet and dry panning, even old stream beds and washes can be made to produce gold. Built-in riffle traps can be depended upon to trap gold whether water is present or not. True, dry panning takes more time than wet panning and requires more practice. It can be sometimes more profitable, however, because dry streams that have not seen water for many years — or centuries — can sometimes be especially productive since they were probably passed by during the busier gold rush days. Old timers, remember, with less efficient metal pans, preferred to work with running water because panning there was easier. You may be the very first person ever to pan for gold in a specific desert location. That fact alone can make a trip to the gold fields worthwhile.

Finding a beauty such as this is a rare feat for any hobbyist, but the large nugget is typical of those that can be found in nature with a modern detector.

Today's electronic detection equipment and improved pans are discovering new gold-producing areas daily, and the known producing areas of the past are giving up gold deposits that the old timers overlooked. Fun, excitement and profit of recreational mining are waiting in beautiful gold country. Treasure hunters of today are limited only by desire and time.

Lightweight Dredges

Crude gold dredges, ugly in appearance and often bigger than a house, have been used for gold recovery since before the turn of the century. Dredging is by far the easiest way to retrieve gold from river and stream gravels. Yet, the tools of dredging have been improved for the weekend or recreational prospector just like the gold pan. Today's modern lightweight suction dredges are capable of working bedrock cracks and crevices almost with the speed and efficiency of an underwater vacuum cleaner. And, they are simple enough to be operated by a single person.

Powered by a small gasoline engine which drives a centrifugal pump to create the vacuum needed to suck up sand, rock, gravel and other gold-bearing materials from stream beds, dredges for today's recreational miner are extremely efficient and light enough to be packed into wilderness locations by one man. The sluice box of the dredge is designed to retain even fine gold, yet spill large rocks and other materials back into the water without clogging the riffles. Ease of cleanup depends upon the size and type of dredge used.

Dredge operation is simple. The hose, which can range from 1 1/2 to 6 inches in diameter, is worked slowly along the bottom of a stream, with its suction chewing away at a gravel bank. Some gold can be recovered from the gravel, but the richest deposits are usually trapped in crevices of the bedrock itself beneath an overburden of sand, silt and gravel. Suction is usually sufficient — with the use of a crevicing tool — to reach ever deeper toward bedrock, breaking up jammed gravel in cracks and cleaning the rich deposits of fine gold and nuggets out of the crevices.

Material is pulled up through the hose and dumped onto the riffles in the sluice box that floats on the surface. Flow of water keeps sand, rocks and lighter material moving along the riffles until they drop out of the opposite end of the box into the water. Heavier gold flakes and nuggets are trapped behind the riffles where they remain until the concentrates are panned down, usually at the end of the day or after dredging ceases.

Before you use a suction dredge in a river or stream, check with local authorities concerning its legality. Some states require a dredging permit. In California it is obtainable at the local office of the Department of Fish and Game. Other states prohibit dredge operation in certain locations.

Restrictions on this equipment were enacted because the huge, old dredges moved great mountains of sand and gravel. Some irresponsible operators left ugly scars on the countryside that are still visible. It's unfortunate that their lack of concern for our environment should prohibit a recreational miner from using a small dredge today since the smaller models cause no ecological harm. Indeed, all material removed from a streambed is returned immediately to it! In fact, this turnover of the stream's bottom serves a worthwhile purpose since it provides new supplies of food for fish and other forms of marine life.

Yes, operations of the gigantic old dredges often left huge stacks of rocks and mud piled alongside streams, producing not only an eyesore but also, in some cases, actually changing the course of the stream itself. Always remember, however, that these eyesores can lead you to wealth that can be discovered with your metal detector. Oftentimes, solid gold nuggets and gold enclosed in large mudballs passed through the dredges and were dumped out with tailings. Your modern metal detector can locate this gold missed by the early day dredgers. The subject of searching dredge piles is discussed in more detail in Chapters Ten and Twelve.

Chapter 4

Finding Gold
Is Not So Difficult...

an I find gold nuggets with a metal detector?" This is the question that we hear most often from gold seekers who doubt their ability — or anyone's ability, for that matter — to find gold with a detector. Surprisingly enough, the question often comes from veterans of the hobby — real treasure hunters, if you will — who certainly have found many coins and gold rings in parks, on beaches and elsewhere. They doubt the ability of any detector in the gold fields.

Of course, the answer to the question is a most emphatic, "*yes!*" Metal detectors are designed specifically to locate metal, and gold is a metal.

Moreover, we have proved, many times over, the abilities of metal detectors for finding gold nuggets in the field. Some of our results and those of others are included in this book.

It is true that advertising and promotional claims of some detector manufacturers have been misleading and have led hobbyists to disappointment. Unfortunately, some metal detector enthusiasts became convinced that they could rush out into a gold-producing area with *any* type of detector and find nuggets and placer gold. Their efforts led mostly to disappointment.

It is possible that those individuals who manufactured and/or sold the so-called *gold-finding* detectors simply did not understand the limitations of their instruments. Let us hope that naivete alone explains the situation!

The fact of the matter is that until almost the 1980's the Beat Frequency Oscillator (BFO) detector was the only type that could be depended upon to produce consistent and accurate readings, as far as gold is concerned. The BFO itself, however, was and continues to be quite limited because of its marginal depth penetration in mineralized ground. And, any longtime detectorist will inform you about the high degree of skill required to maximize performance of a BFO detector.

Today's ground-canceling (balancing) detectors offer greatly expanded capabilities:

— Detection depth has been tremendously increased, particularly with the highly regarded 15 kHz "Groundhog" circuit;

— Ground mineral problems have been mostly overcome;

— Rapid and accurate identification of "hot rocks" is possible, even for the beginner.

As a result of extensive field and laboratory tests and careful electronic design and manufacturing techniques, detectors possessing very exacting metal/mineral locating and identifying characteristics are now being built. Using these tested and proven detectors, both professional and recreational prospectors are making rich strikes in previously unworked areas, unearthing nuggets similar to those found at the turn of the century.

Significant recent gold and silver strikes include:

— In North Georgia Bill Boye found a gold-filled quartz specimen weighing almost 17 1/2 pounds, the largest single find in Georgia since the height of its gold rush of the early 1800s.

— Jason Martin discovered a nugget weighing 125 troy ounces in Australia and named it the "Centenary Nugget."

— In central Washington Roy Lagal (one of the authors) found a 2 1/2-pound gold nugget.

— Using a 12 1/2-inch Crossfire searchcoil, Kevin J. Clark of Newcomb, Australia, detected a 5 1/2-ounce nugget at a depth of 20 inches.

— A metal detector operator reports that he found a beautiful 36-ounce gold nugget near the central Cascade Mountains in Washington.

— Charles Garrett (the other author) spent several weeks prospecting in Mexico; in one mine alone Charles found two large pockets and one vein of silver.

— A 47-ounce nugget found at Mt. Magnet, Western Australia, although valued at "only" $7,000 for its gold content, was appraised at $25,000 as a specimen.

— A 25-ounce nugget and a 36-ounce nugget were found with detectors in northeastern Australian gold fields.

— Peter Bridge of Victoria Park, Western Australia, reports that more than 1000 pounds of gold nuggets have been found by his customers using detectors.

— Two hundred ounces of small nuggets were recovered by two prospectors in Western Australia. One detector operator, working alone, found more than 500 ounces of large gold nuggets.

— After a gold panning weekend in Georgia, Pam Wendel Clayton returned home with a vial of beautiful, tiny gold nuggets.

— The most magnificent find of all may be the 62-pound Hand of Faith nugget found in Australia by an amateur prospector using a detector with the Groundhog circuit. This nugget was reportedly sold for one million dollars to the Gold Nugget Casino in Las Vegas, Nevada, where it was put on display.

Australian Gold

When a single man, equipped with only a ground-canceling metal detector, finds more than 500 ounces of gold in a few short months, metal detector hobbyists everywhere should take notice. A small-scale recreational mining boom has occurred in Australia, and recreational prospectors the world over have shown interest. Peter Bridge, who owns and operates a prospector's supply house in Western Australia, was largely responsible for introducing the modern metal detector to that continent.

Although no "official" data is available concerning the overall results of the Australian boom, a newspaper in Perth reported, "It is estimated that more than 2,000 ounces of alluvial gold was picked up by Western Australian prospectors" in just the first two years.

This new Australian gold rush is attributed to two major factors:

— Banking (gold) regulations were repealed, enabling gold to be sold on the open market in Australia;

— Sophisticated metal detectors were introduced by Peter Bridge and others to give Australian prospectors a highly efficient gold-finding tool.

The State of Washington

Roy and Charles joined Frank Duval at Liberty, Washington, to search the old dredge tailings, conveyor piles and mine pits for nuggets and rich ore deposits. Even though that area of the country is very highly mineralized, results produced by new ground-balancing detectors proved truly amazing.

"Mining in this district has been described as different from any other mining district in the world," Roy Mayo writes in his book *Give Me Liberty*. "Placer gold has been found as water-worn, rounded nuggets, indicating travel over a long distance. Nuggets have also been found having sharp edges with pieces of quartz still attached, indicating nearness to the source. Flakes of gold and delicate wire gold are also found. This is one of the few places in the world where gold may be found in its crystalline form."

Lode gold can also be found around Liberty. Shale and clay pockets contain delicate wire gold as well as gold in other forms in stringers in the sandstone and in a mixture of quartz and shale that is known as "birds-eye quartz." Major area discoveries of wire gold have been made on Flag Mountain and Snowshoe Ridge, according to Mayo. Many beautiful specimens of wire gold weighing several pounds have been found there.

We have found gold numerous times with a metal detector in the Liberty area. Because of its wide variety both in types of gold deposits and in types of hunting, it offers an unusual challenge. We worked old dredge tailings where large nuggets have been found by eyesight alone over the years by casual vacationers and picnickers. We also checked for pockets of wire gold on Mrs. Bertha Benson's claim on Flag Mountain and pinpointed both non-magnetic conductive ore veins and magnetic non-conductive ore veins as well. All of these activities were coordinated by Jacob Kirsch, who has been mining claims in the Liberty area for many years.

Working dredge piles along Swauk Creek was a real eye-opener. After we first carefully regulated the ground balance of our detectors to cancel out existing ground mineralization, we swept the instruments slowly over large boulders, searching for elusive gold nuggets that escaped the trommel of the dredge many years ago.

This book has said little yet of "hot rocks," but it is a subject about which you will hear much more. On this pile of dredge tailings in Washington we really discovered the true meaning of the term. They can be defined basically as those out-of-place, highly mineralized rocks that try to fool even the circuitry of even the best metal detectors. Hobbyists can get in big trouble, indeed, if they are not alert to them. As we scanned these tailings, we encountered countless numbers of hot rocks, but easily identified them with the calibrated discriminating capabilities of our modern Garrett detectors. We worked a considerable area of those tailings, but the end results of the day's electronic prospecting were well worth the trouble.

On the hill above Liberty we carefully searched for pockets of gold and highly mineralized veins on a rich hardrock claim that has produced many thousands of dollars in gold. A number of veins were discovered and mapped out to be excavated and examined at a later date for precious metals. Initial findings proved conclusively that metal detectors with ground balance capable of being properly adjusted to cancel out mineralization can be of enormous benefit to any prospector. In fact, we are convinced that it is the most important tool that a weekend miner or recreational prospector can own. Used properly, the detector can find conductive (non-ferrous) and non-conductive (predominantly magnetic) deposits, as well as nuggets, pockets and veins of all kinds wherever sufficient quantities of magnetic iron are present.

Chapter 5

Gold Pan
Basic Recovery Tool...

Gold pans and gold panning methods have remained basically unchanged for many thousands of years. Because gold is almost 20 times as heavy as water, it will sink rapidly and is easily recovered by "panning." Various panning methods have been used over the centuries, and many different types of vessels have been employed.

Yet regardless of the vast span of time that gold has been coveted as wealth, the methods of recovering it by panning remain essentially the same. Any pan, bowl or container made of any type of material — even a blanket — can be used to recover the heavy metal. In water it can be panned easily or sorted from lighter rocks and dirt because gold is heavier and tends to sink quickly down through all the debris, finally coming to rest at the bottom. Gold can also be recovered by dry methods where water is not available; however, this "dry" washing or panning is not as efficient, and generally only the heavier pieces can be recovered without sophisticated equipment.

Illustrated step-by-step instructions for panning with water — by far the most common method — follow this chapter. And, a new gold recovery device is now available to make it even easier to pan. Since we're talking primarily about metal detectors in this book, however, let's discuss how a pan should be used with them.

Many times a plastic gold pan can spell the difference between arduous digging and abandoning a target that has fallen down into a large pile of gravel or rocks. No matter what your target in a heap of rocks or flowing stream proves to be, a plastic pan makes its recovery much faster and easier.

The technique is simple. First, of course, pay close attention to the faintest signals from your detector. They may indicate that the nuggets are small or that they are deeply buried. Second, you must pinpoint each detector response as closely as you can. Then, slip a shovel well under the spot from which the signal came. Be extremely careful now since small objects made of heavy metal can become loose and be lost when they sink into gravel. Carefully place into your plastic gold pan all of the gravel or sand that you scooped up, and scan this sample with your detector.

The value of having a *plastic* pan is now apparent. It would be impossible to scan the sample if the pan were made of metal.

In the plastic pan any conductive target will respond when you scan it. If there is no response, dump the pan and scan the location again until your detector repeats its signals. Pinpoint your target and try to get under it again with your shovel. With a bit of practice, you will be surprised at how quickly you can become proficient in this technique — even when working in three feet of running water!

Your techniques of recovery using a plastic pan are the same when searching a dry wash or placer diggings, except the object will be easier to pinpoint than when submerged in a stream. Old dredge tailings may be somewhat more difficult in which to locate targets, and you may lose a few here before you master the technique. Material in which you are working is loose, and an object of heavier metal can easily and quickly work its way deeper into the pile of tailings. Once lost, they are often very difficult or impossible to find since they simply fall deeper into the pile with each attempt you make to recover them.

You will be tempted to give up in frustration and move to a new location. On the other hand, you'll be surprised at how quickly you become proficient and tenacious at such recoveries once you realize that the metallic object you are seeking just might be a gold nugget!

Now let's talk about pans themselves!

Remember the old prospector from the Western movies riding his decrepit burro across Monument Valley into a beautiful Hollywood sunset? All he had was a skillet or pie pan with which he scooped up gravel and panned for gold. Of course, he needed more equipment than that (a shovel or digging tool, certainly), but as far as the pan was concerned, the depiction is still more or less accurate.

Pan designs have improved greatly since the old prospector's time. Today's gold pan is lighter in weight and offers greater speed in testing and classifying concentrates. It is also easier to handle and provides safer, surer results.

Of course, we believe the finest and most effective gold pans today to be the Gravity Trap pans. Invented by Roy (U.S. Patent #4,162,969) and manufactured by Charles' company, its effectiveness has been proven by worldwide success and acceptance. Made of unbreakable polypropylene, the pans are far lighter and easier to handle than metal pans. More importantly, the Gravity Trap pan has built-in gold traps in the form of sharp 90° riffles. These riffles are designed to trap the heavier gold and allow fast panning-off of unwanted sand, rocks and gravel. They allow you to retain gold that might be discarded from another pan. Absolutely no experience is required for a beginner to enjoy success in the first panning session with a Gravity Trap pan.

Now a new and improved device is available. It's called the Garrett Super Sluice because that's exactly what it is — a hand-held sluice. Fifteen inches in diameter, it can handle a greater volume of material and increase recovery speed dramatically. Because the riffles are twice as deep as those in the smaller Gravity Trap pans, they will do an even better job of trapping nuggets both large and small, as well as particles of gold.

All Gravity Trap pans and the Super Sluice are forest green in color which has been proved in laboratory and field tests to show gold, garnets, precious gems and black sand better than other colors, including black. After only a little practice, a recreational panner using Gravity Trap pans can work with equal or greater efficiency than the most proficient professional using old style metal pans or those of black plastic design.

During the gold rush days of the 19th and early 20th centuries, gold panning was more than hard work; it was back-breaking labor. Unless a panner was lucky, it was usually not especially profitable. Today, however, gold panning is much easier and far more productive. This has happened not only because of the increased price of gold but because of the Gravity Trap gold pans that make panning so much quicker and simpler. And, the new device now available makes panning even easier!

Since Gravity Trap pans can be used for both wet and dry panning, even old stream beds and washes can be made to produce gold. Built-in riffle traps will trap gold whether water is present or not. True, dry panning takes longer than wet panning and requires more practice. It can be sometimes more profitable, however, because dry streams that have not seen water for many years — or centuries — can sometimes be especially productive. They were probably passed by during the busier gold rush days because old timers with less efficient metal pans preferred to work with running water since panning there was so much easier. You may be the *first* person ever to pan in a productive waterless location!

Chapter 6

The Detector

A Gold-Finding Tool...

The modern metal detector is essentially a product of the computer age. Until the 1980s detectors were relatively simple instruments. No longer. Modern gold-finders such as Garrett's GTI and Infinium LS detectors rely heavily on computer science.

True, the history of these instruments can be traced back many decades...even centuries, if folklore is to be believed. Speaking personally, Roy began using military metal detectors during World War II. Charles used the war surplus instruments shortly afterward, and lack of success with them led him to developing his own designs more than 40 years ago.

So, given this history, how can we state flatly that the metal detector is a product of the computer age?

Our statement concerns the metal detector *as we know it today.*

The 21st Century metal detector is as different from those of just 15 years ago as Boeing's latest jet aircraft is from the glorified kite that Orville Wright "flew" for 30 yards at Kitty Hawk more than a century ago. Anyone still trying to use a detector built before about 1990 is struggling with an antique, no matter how effectively it may seem to perform. That's not to say that the early detectors didn't do a job of finding metal. We won World War II with the mine detectors of that era. And, speaking

Gold Panning Instructions

1. Place the classifier atop the large gold pan and fill with sand and gravel shoveled from bedrock.

2. Submerge the classifier contents under water and use a firm, twisting motion to loosen material. Gold, sand and small gravel will pass through the classifier into your gold pan. Check for nuggets in the classifier and watch for mud or clay balls that might contain nuggets.

3. Discard all material remaining in classifier. Use your hands to loosen all material in the gold pan thoroughly. Inspect contents and remove pebbles. With the pan completely submerged or all contents of the pan under water twist it with a rotating motion to permit the heavy gold to sink to the bottom.

4. Always keep the contents submerged. Continue the rotating, shaking motion. From time to time tip the pan forward to permit water to carry off lighter material. Pour over the Gravity Trap riffles so that gold can sink into them.

5. As you shake the pan to agitate the contents make certain that the pan remains completely submerged or that all material in it is always under water. Remember that the Gravity Trap riffles should be on the downside whenever the pan is tilted. As lighter material floats over the pan's edge, riffles will trap the heavier gold. Rake off larger rocks and pebbles from time to time.

2

3

4

5

6

7

8

9

10

6. Develop a method of agitation with which you are comfortable. Back and forth... round and round... or, whatever suits you. Your aim is to settle and retain the heavy gold while letting the lighter material wash across the riffles and out of the pan. As contents of the pan diminish, smooth and gentle motions are mandatory. Use extreme care in pouring lighter material over the side. Submerge pan often and tilt it backward to let water return all material to the bottom of the pan.

7. If there is a larger than usual concentration of black sand, you may wish to transfer the material to the smaller finishing pan for speedier separation.

8. Continue the panning motion to let all remaining lighter material flow off the edge.

9. Now, you can retain the black sand concentrates or continue gentle motions to let it ease off the edge of the pan. As visual identification becomes possible, a gentle swirling motion will leave your gold concentrated together.

10. Retrieve your gold. Use tweezers for the larger pieces and the suction bottle to vacuum fine gold from the small amount of water you permitted to remain in the pan. Save the remaining black sand for later milling and further classification at home.

personally again, we found a lot of treasure with metal detectors in the 1960s and 1970s and witnessed a lot more being found by others. Plus, the first primitive detectors represented a definite improvement for the ancient activity of prospecting for precious metals. The first detector Charles ever designed is in the Garrett Museum, and we guarantee that either of us could take it out today and find gold nuggets with it.

Yet the modern metal detectors we are manufacturing just a short distance west of the Garrett Museum are truly space age products. Their performance is heavily dependent upon computers, both in controls and the analysis of data. Thus, the advancement in metal detectors is related directly to the great strides forward that have been made in computer technology.

In fact, most modern microprocessor-controlled detectors can do far more than their operators ever ask of them — just as most computers can do far more than they are ever called on to do. Still and all, searching for precious metal is just one of the detector uses that has benefited from these great technological advances.

Exactly *what* can a metal detector bring to the search for gold?

To answer that question let's first reflect for a moment on the 19th-century gold prospectors…and, not just the hardships they endured and the difficult conditions under which they worked. Consider their tools. They really had no equipment to help them find and identify gold other than their eyes. If they could not actually see the gold itself or recognize gold-bearing rocks, they would emerge from their struggle with nature without any color or nuggets.

On the other hand, today's gold-seeker — whether he is working full-time at the task or only on weekends and vacations — carries the electronic metal detector as a valuable prospecting tool. Sensitive, lightweight, stable and reliable, today's metal detector serves as an "extra pair of eyes" for the modern prospector.

These detectors can find gold in a number of forms:

— Lode or hard rock deposits in a vein and often mixed with other materials;

— Placer deposits, either in a stream or in dry sands and gravel;

— Nuggets of pure metal, which can be found in nature by themselves, in veins or as part of a placer deposit.

Placer gold is the type most often sought after by the weekend prospector who enters the gold fields only with a panning kit. Yet more and more hobbyists are now taking detectors with them to search for nuggets and rich lode deposits as well. Plus, the detectors can help them locate deposits of placer gold.

These placer deposits are generally formed by weather erosion of an outcropping of lode gold. After the outcropping has become exposed over the years and decades, it begins to break apart and smaller pieces crumble off. Gravity and water run off carry them downhill. Some of these pieces of ore still lie on mountainsides awaiting a metal detector. Most of them, however, are carried by water down into streams where larger chunks are ground into smaller particles of sand and gravel, thus releasing gold from the lode. Because of its comparatively heavy weight, gold sinks and works its way down vertically to bedrock of the stream where it is trapped in cracks or crevices while the lighter sand and gravel are swept on by rushing waters.

While most placer gold was originally deposited by water, nature's changes over the centuries have left many good placer deposits high and dry. Sand washes in gold-producing country sometimes contain a high concentration of fine or so-called flour gold that can be recovered by dry panning or by use of a dry washer. It is not unusual to find, mixed in with placer gold, small nuggets that can be easily detected with a good metal detector.

Finding vein or lode gold with a metal detector can be more difficult. Generally, extensive experience or considerable research is required if the weekend miner is to be successful in developing new locations. Knowledge of geology is helpful, but the inexperienced prospector can often be quite successful simply by working around abandoned mines and mine dumps where others have successfully extracted gold from nature. Many times, the early day miners would miss a rich ore vein by just inches and leave the location, considering it barren. Because they had only eyesight to guide them, these pioneer gold seekers would often follow a vein far into a mountain, digging just inches away from an incredibly richer vein they could not see. Your modern metal detector when worked along the walls of these old mine tunnels may reveal the precise location of that rich vein the earlier miners overlooked.

Today's weekend prospector finds all the hard work of moving tons and tons of earth already completed. In fact, by examining just the few inches behind walls, roof and floor of a mine, the recreational miner can prospect more cubic yardage in just a few hours than the old miners could in months.

Similarly, dumps and tailing piles of old mines are good locations to work. They are certainly the easiest and quickest sources of gold if the prospector knows how to use a detector properly. Large gold or silver nuggets can be found concealed within a chunk of rock that was unknowingly discarded on the dump. The old-time miner could not see the valuable material hidden by the rock, but a metal detector can certainly signal its presence.

In Cobalt, Ontario, Canada, Charles located several large chunks of silver that were apparently discarded accidentally 50 years ago along with worthless material that was used to build a roadbed. The largest piece of ore he detected weighed 50 pounds and consisted of 85 percent silver.

Never pass up the opportunity to work discards in the tailing piles around abandoned mines. Many times more gold is still in the ground that was recovered by the early miners. It is yours for the taking!

Chapter 7

Which Detectors
Find Gold Best?

This is a book relating essentially how we and others have found gold in various forms by using the *right* metal detector and using it properly. We hope to share these experiences…to leave a clear idea of how you too can find gold with a detector. This book is not a metal detector handbook or training manual. Yet, the facts are we've proved that metal detectors *can* find gold. And, you are reading this book because you are interested in the type of detectors that we believe to be best for discovering gold.

There are a number of metal detectors on the market today that are advertised as suitable for finding gold. Those of you who are familiar with Charles Garrett's writing, however, know that he discusses only Garrett detectors. There are distinct reasons for this, and none of them is concerned with "touting" his company's products. In fact, Charles often hears compliments about the limited amount of sales effort contained in these books. No, the authors will write about Garrett detectors because we know and understand them. Sure, either of us can find gold with any properly designed detector. But, since we don't have the experience with competitive brands that we have with Garrett, we wouldn't be able to stress their strong points. And, for us to criticize a Garrett competitor's product would be presumptions indeed!

Any Garrett detector can be used to look for gold, and we are confident that you will enjoy some success with any of them, if used patiently and properly. But, just as you would want the proper rifle or shotgun for hunting game, you want the right detector for hunting gold.

What we are saying is that with Garrett's automatic GTAx models or its Treasure Aces — each of which is among the finest instruments in the world for finding coins and jewelry — you might miss out on flakes or tiny nuggets. If you will use the detectors we're about to discuss (or similar detectors from other manufacturers), you will give yourself a much better chance of actually recovering any gold that you might encounter.

Please remember that *all* detectors are *not* suitable for gold-hunting — regardless of advertising claims or cost. Just because a detector is expensive doesn't make it a "universal" instrument. Investigate before you buy!

Garrett produces several detectors that are uniquely equipped to help you hunt successfully for gold. Our principal gold-finder is the Scorpion Gold Stinger which offers numerous features that will be discussed in this book. Also available from Garrett are the Master Hunter CX and GTI 2500 detectors, computerized models with microprocessor controls. They offer the deepseeking all metal mode required for finding gold as well as the discriminate mode so popular with coin hunters.

Garrett's brand new (for the 21st century) Infinium LS is an outstanding detector for experienced gold-hunters, especially those who search in heavily mineralized ground where gold is usually found. Advanced Pulse Induction (API) technology ignores hot rocks and overall changing ground mineralization while reaching the industry's greatest depth to find gold nuggets. We urge you to investigate and consider this marvelous new detector.

The Scorpion, CX and GTI detectors are truly universal instruments that can be used to hunt for coins, jewelry or anything else when you aren't finding gold! When you select a new detector, we urge a close investigation of the "multi-purpose" aspects of any instrument you consider. Before you purchase a detector that offers *only* a Deep-seeking all metal mode with no discrimination capability, ask yourself this question: "Will I be using this detector to hunt *only* for gold?" An honest answer may help you avoid the frustration of trying to hunt for coins (or, watching your wife try to hunt for coins) with a detector that has no Discriminate mode.

What Is A Detector?

It's not necessary to understand the scientific principles of metal detection to use a detector to hunt for gold. You can find nuggets, float, veins and other forms of the precious metal without knowing how a detector works. For better comprehension of what a metal detector is doing, however...to recognize why it just made that *peculiar* sound...to understand why it reacts the way it does to metals and minerals...it is helpful to learn the facts of metal detector operation.

Now, if you're a metal detector expert or if you've read other books by either of the authors, you might want to skip this. But, we suggest you read on. We would... because we never know what we can learn from reading and studying some more about something we think we already know! And, the physical *laws* and the mythical *lore* of treasure hunting and metal detecting never change...just the personalities involved and their experiences.

We generally begin explaining what a detector *is* by pointing out what it is *not*. It's not an instrument (Geiger counter) that detects energy emissions from radioactive materials. It's not an instrument (magnetometer) that measures the intensity of magnetic fields. It doesn't "point" to coins, jewelry or any other kind of metal; it doesn't measure the abundance of metal. A metal detector simply detects the presence of metal and reports this fact.

Metal is detected essentially by the transmission and reception of radio wave signals. When a detector is turned on, a radio signal is transmitted from its coil (antenna), generating an electromagnetic field that flows out into any surrounding medium, whether it be earth, rock, water, wood, coral, air or any other material. The extent of this field, and the depth to which a nugget or other metallic item can be detected depends upon the type of searchcoil, power used to transmit the radio signal and the resistance of the medium into which the signal is transmitted. Metal detection occurs, then, when the electromagnetic lines encounter metal.

This penetration causes electrical eddy currents to flow on the metal's surface. The generation of these currents results in a power loss in the electromagnetic field. Another effect occurs when the very presence of metal distorts the detector's electromagnetic field and changes its shape.

This loss of power and the resulting distortion of the electromagnetic field are sensed by the metal detector. When circuitry of the metal detector simultaneously interprets all these sensations, it signals to the operator that some type of metallic object is present.

Quite simply, the quality of signals generated, received and interpreted by the metal detector and the ability of the hobbyist to act upon them determines the difference between "digging junk" and finding a gold nugget.

Yet, soil directly beneath a searchcoil that a metal detector "illuminates" through transmission of signals usually contains numerous elements and minerals...some detectable and some not, some desirable and some not. A metal detector's electronic response at any given instant is caused by all conductive metals and minerals and ferrous non-conductive minerals located in the "illuminated" area. And, some minerals and metals may be worthless.

Two of the most undesirable minerals are also two of the most common: natural iron (ferrous minerals) found in much of the earth's soil and wetted salt that is often prevalent in the earth's soil and water. Not only do these minerals produce detection signals, but they inhibit the ability of detectors to find metal.

When iron minerals are present, the electromagnetic field is upset and signals are distorted similar to the distortion when metal is detected. Iron mineral detection, therefore, has always presented a major problem to manufacturers and users of metal detectors. Although detection of such minerals may be desirable when a you're seeking ferrous "black sand" that could contain gold or silver, it is a nuisance to you when you're looking for nuggets or any other kind of treasure.

A primary design criterion of any detector, therefore, must be to filter or eliminate responses from undesirable elements, informing the treasure hunter only of those from desirable objects. This is accomplished in a variety of ways depending upon the type of metal detector. If you ever get serious about studying mineralization, target identification, field applications and other subjects, you'll want to learn more about this subject. In some of Charles' other books, especially *Modern Metal Detectors*, he discusses at length how Garrett goes about eliminating undesirable mineral detection. All you *have* to do right now, however, is purchase a new high quality detector. You'll never be faced with this problem.

Depth of Detection

How deep can a metal detector find gold or any other kind of metal? When an electromagnetic field flows out of the searchcoil, several factors determine whether detection is possible: electromagnetic field strength, target size, surface area of the target and the type of metal in the target. How far the electromagnetic field flows from the searchcoil also depends on the size of the searchcoil, quality of its construction and materials that are present in the earth. Larger searchcoils produce a larger field that can penetrate more deeply to detect deeper treasures.

It is realistic to expect that a coin-sized target can be detected under normal conditions to depths of at least six to nine inches. Of course, a "coin-sized" nugget would be a great find indeed. Since most nuggets you encounter will probably be somewhat smaller, you cannot expect them to be detected as deeply as larger objects.

Of course, the Australian mentioned in Chapter 4 reported using his Grand Master Hunter CX II with a 12 1/2-inch coil to detect a 5 1/2-ounce nugget at a depth of some 20 inches. Incredible!

Still, there are so many factors involved with detection depth that nuggets of any size can often be found deeper than anticipated and, sometimes, shallower...all because of such variables as ground mineralization, atmospheric conditions and the like. Gold is a reasonably good conductor, however, and a modern detector can be expected to find even small traces of it. The shape and orientation of your nugget can have an effect on depth of detection. Metal detectors are, for the most part, surface area detectors. They are not metallic volume (mass) detectors. The larger the surface area of a metal target that is "looking at" the bottom of the searchcoil, the better and deeper that target will be detected.

How Detectors "Report"

When a treasure hunter is scanning his searchcoil over the ground or in the water, a detector reports information on targets in three ways:

– Increases or decreases in audible volume (universal on all detectors);

– Graphic information presented on LCD meters (sometimes reported in a numerical "code");

– Meter deflections (types of meters can vary greatly, along with the amount and accuracy of the information they present).

Acceptable objects cause the audio or meter indicators to increase in amplitude; unacceptable objects cause the indicators to decrease, or the objects are ignored. Detectors with LCD indicators, such as Garrett's GTA models and the CX III, will provide even more information concerning the possible value of targets.

Learn to listen closely to your detector's signals, and interpret what is being "told" to you through sound and meter/LCD indicators. This discussion is essentially continued in the following chapters which tell more about the various methods that we recommend be used to search for gold with a metal detector.

Some detectors will barely detect a fair-sized nugget one inch deep, yet others will detect that same nugget at extreme depths. A most important factor, therefore, in successful detector operation is the expertise and ability of the operator. Metal detector manufacturers get letters from customers who complain about finding nothing but hot rocks with their detector. Yet, other letters bubble over with enthusiasm and joy because the writers are finding gold *with the very same detectors*. Accompanying photographs often offer further testimony to all that they have found.

What is the difference? Certainly, it doesn't lie in the capability of the detector. One can obviously take identical instruments and place them in the hands of different people with entirely different results.

There is no doubt in our minds that as long as it performs basic functions, a poorly built detector will produce more in the hands of an experienced hobbyist than a high quality detector will in the hands of a person who does not understand the instrument or know how to use it.

The best advice we can give you about any metal detector is perhaps the most obvious. *Read your instruction manual!* Yes, that's right...carefully read and study the operator's manual that accompanied your detector. In fact, at Garrett we recommend that you study this manual *before* you purchase a detector. If the manufacturer has "skimped" on providing instructions and advice, you might find your gold-hunting success similarly shorted.

On the other hand, an extremely detailed manual that you find hard to understand could well indicate a detector that's going to prove complicated and difficult to learn how to use. Such an instrument might also become one that you can easily *forget* how to use when you haven't hunted for some time. You don't want a detector so complicated that to have to read an instruction manual continually.

At Garrett we believe that our computerized, microprocessor-controlled detectors should be *simple to use*, not difficult. Our Owner's Manuals will reveal this to you. If some other manual contains a massive number of pages and diagrams to explain its "simplicity," be wary of the detector it describes.

Above all, a hobbyist must develop trust in his or her metal detector and become "one" with it. Together you can comprise an unbeatable gold-finding team. The instrument will never lie; you can be confident that it will report exactly what it *sees*. It's up to the hobbyist to interpret the detector's report and recover gold or any other treasure that it discovers. It's a fact that most detector "troubles" are not the fault of the instrument but, rather, the operator's failure to learn to use the equipment properly.

Place your complete trust in a quality metal detector to help you find gold...just as you trust your automobile and other mechanical and electronic devices you use regularly. Believe us when we tell you that you can be richly rewarded. The results are up to you.

Chapter 8

How to Detect

Gold With a Metal Detector...

We urge you to follow four basic rules for prospecting with a metal detector. Now, this will not guarantee your success; nor, even when success comes, will it be achieved instantly. If you follow these rules, however, and are persistent, we have no doubt about your ability to locate and identify any precious metals you encounter:

1. Select the *proper type* of detector. We refer, of course, to the operating characteristics of the detector rather than the brand name. We believe that a detector with a Deepseeking all medal mode is a must. The new Garrett Scorpion Gold Stinger, and its legendary predecessors with the Groundhog circuit that have found tens of thousands of ounces of gold in the United States, Australia and around the world. We recommend it, along with any of Garrett's new CX-type detectors with their microprocessor-controlled, computerized circuitry preprogrammed at the factory. The Stinger and the CX detectors are capable of locating even pinhead-size nuggets and will also identify hot rocks properly. These detectors have the two circuits that are a must for metal vs. mineral identification.

2. You must learn *patience*...with your detector as well as with yourself. Because finding gold is rarely easy, it will take time and effort. You should understand your detector and its capabilities fully. Also, learn the instrument's limitations so that you can become truly proficient in its use. Read this book carefully. Also read the Owner's Manual supplied with your detector. After you have practiced with your detector, read both books again and study them more carefully. To be successful with a metal detector it is essential that you understand the instrument thoroughly, as well as all of the techniques for using it that are described in this book.

Take your Owner's Manual in the field with you for on-the-scene research. You'll find a Garrett manual is printed in a convenient size that will fit into a shirt pocket. We want you to take it with you!

3. Begin your search where gold is *known* to exist. Don't kid yourself here! The preceding sentences are two of the most important in this book. It is impossible to find gold or any other precious metals where they simply do not exist. Prospectors who have found gold with metal detectors have demonstrated wisdom and patience, plus a great deal of *research.* Stick to known, productive mining areas until you are familiar with your detector's operation and understand how it signals the presence of mineral zones. Soon you will discover many other ways in which a quality metal detector can open up completely new areas of success for the you as a recreational miner and prospector.

4. Let us repeat again the importance of *persistence.* Gold may be "easy" to find, but it's almost always very difficult to recover because only minute traces of it often exist and the nuggets are tiny. Do not expect to take your detector into the gold field and begin finding nuggets easily. Do not expect color to appear easily in your pan. You'll have to work hard for it...but, we think it's worth the effort because the more you use your detector and gold pan correctly, the greater your success will be!

The 'Right' Detector

The ideal metal detector that will enable you to achieve the greatest success for prospecting is a sensitive, deep-seeking instrument that has been designed for prospecting and proved in field use. This will be an instrument with a Deepseeking all metal operating mode. Such a mode will offer precise (usually adjustable in the field) ground balance. Properly calibrated discrimination circuitry is also a must. Your gold-hunting detector should contain the necessary circuits for metal vs. mineral determination and hot rock identification. With power to penetrate the toughest iron mineralization, it should have the availability of a complete range of searchcoils from about 4 1/2 inches in diameter to more than 12 inches, both circular and elliptical.

Garrett's Scorpion Gold Stinger offers multi-turn controls for both ground balance and audio threshold and a discrimination control for metal vs. mineral identification. These permit the extremely precise adjustment demanded in heavily mineralized areas. Nearly identical ground balancing and detection characteristics are offered on the entire line of Garrett's CX-type detectors, all of which are ideal for prospecting. Furthermore, the computerized controls of these CX instruments are available to help with ground balancing.

What should such a *capable* ground-balancing metal detector — one that will find gold — cost? Answering a question with a question, we might respond, "What should a car cost?" The answers to both questions are the same. The price will depend on the quality of the product and the features (options) it offers. And it is probably more important to rely on a dependable manufacturer when purchasing a detector than when buying a car.

We believe that each of the major detector manufacturers now offers at least one instrument described as especially designed for finding gold. In addition, some other detectors also provide the manual ground balancing which many who search for gold prefer in certain situations. These detectors obviously vary somewhat in price and, certainly, in ability. As a rule of thumb, however, a gold-hunting detector should have a list price between $350 and $500 (in late 1995). Even then, greater performance can be expected with some higher-priced models. Concerning dollars and cents, however, please don't make the very common mistake of thinking that if you look around and choose the highest priced detector, you will be getting the best instrument.

It is possible, to some extent, to use *any* ground-balancing detector to find precious metals. Yet most modern, microprocessor-controlled detectors can be operated even by a beginner in areas where the older models would have proved almost useless in the hands of an expert because of mineral conditions in the soil.

With a less expensive model or one without manual ground balancing and the discrimination necessary for metal vs. mineral identification, your career as a prospector will probably be short and not very sweet. You'll "retire" pretty quickly in discouragement because you won't find gold.

Let's talk about discriminating detectors — those without the Deepseeking all metal mode which requires ground balance. Quality discriminating instruments can be used effectively for nugget hunting. When using such a detector, however, you must resign yourself to the fact that it will overlook tiny nuggets. And, the discrimination controls of this type detector are sometimes not calibrated at the factory for precise metal/mineral discrimination. Even when the controls are set at zero on most discriminating detectors, they continue to provide a minimum amount of discrimination that might cause gold to be lost, especially flakes or tiny nuggets.

Note how this elliptical Crossfire searchcoil can be inserted easily between large rocks to permit scanning closer to the ground where gold is suspected.

Garrett's new GTA detectors are truly automatic instruments that offer the depth of detection that is so important in the gold fields. In addition, however, they provide a distinct advantage to gold hunters. This advantage is *notch discrimination*. Of course, the GTA should be set with zero discrimination whenever it is used for nugget hunting. Some areas, however, contain so much iron trash that a slight amount of discrimination becomes highly desirable, even necessary. It is even possible with the GTA to establish a special "notch" to avoid a single, particularly troublesome junk metal target.

We know that in old mining camps boot nails and eyelets from shoes and boots are often a pesky nuisance to any detector operating in a mode with no discrimination. With the GTA it is possible to search with such targets entirely "notched out."

And, even while using this notch the operator will be able to "see" all targets discovered by the detector. They will be reported visibly on the Graphic Target Analyzer™ even when the detector makes no sound.

It is important to remember that the Scorpion Gold Stinger also offers factory calibration in its discriminate circuits as required for metal vs. mineral identification.

Depending on existing mineral conditions, you might achieve some success in locating nuggets with a quality discriminating detector or with the Stinger in its Discriminate mode. It is highly likely, however, that you will overlook tiny nuggets, ore veins and such that would

When searching dredge piles such as this, using a plastic gold pan to check discoveries will keep a valuable nugget from falling deeper into the rocks.

71

tiny nuggets, ore veins and the like that would be found with the *right type* of detector that permits you to use a Deepseeking all metal mode.

Such an instrument with properly calibrated ground balance and metal vs. mineral identification that has been proved by successful testing and performance in the field will offer superior performance in detecting small and large nuggets and both conductive and non-conductive ore (predominantly magnetic) veins. This is the type of detector that we recommend for finding gold.

Searchcoils

Two types of circular searchcoils are commonly available for use with prospecting instruments, the co-planar loop and the concentric loop. Both searchcoil windings are positioned on the same plane, but only concentric windings are centered around the same vertical axis. Consequently, concentric searchcoils produce a desirable, uniformly distributed electromagnetic field. Fewer irregularities will present themselves when a concentric searchcoil is used.

Almost two decades ago Garrett also produced elliptical searchcoils especially designed to fit into "tight places" that would not accommodate a circular coil. Some of us used them regularly.

Garrett recently introduced two totally new elliptical searchcoils suited for any kind of searching, but especially applicable to the rocky gold fields. These new elliptical coils offer the same searching advantages of the old elliptical coils but hunt deeper and with more precision. They create a "knife-edge" searching matrix and thus pierce deeply into the soil.

Analyzing Ore Samples

Before you take your detector into the field, experiment with it on the bench to learn how it will react to various ore samples. The following chapter discusses making ore samples. If possible, get two grades of various ores for your tests, a very high grade and a very low grade specimen of each. By conducting your own bench analysis you can become familiar with the type and amount of detector response to the various materials.

If the ore you are checking has a predominance of metal in detectable form (use a silver dime for testing), you will hear a sound increase as the sample is moved closer to the searchcoil. If your detector is equipped with a sensitivity meter, you will see a positive pointer movement indicating the presence of metal. On the other hand, if the sound has a tendency to "die" slightly, your sample contains a predominance of mineral or natural magnetic iron (Fe_3O_4). This does not mean that the sample contains *no* metal, only that it contains *more* mineral than it does metal. If the sample contains *neither* metal nor mineral, or if it has electrically *equal* amounts of both, you will receive *no* response on your detector.

Always remember that even the finest metal detectors do *not* respond to many types of ores. Only those ore samples containing metal in conductive form in sufficient quantity to disturb the electromagnetic field will cause the detector to respond positively. You should continually practice bench testing to become more familiar with the type and amount of response your particular detector will give to both low and high grade ores. A little time spent experimenting can save you many hours of confusion when you are in the field — and it may keep you from missing valuable nuggets, ore samples or veins!

Correct identification of metal, mineral and marginal ore samples is critical, and it must be accomplished with the detector in a stable position. Otherwise, you and your detector are guessing. Detectors that discriminate or reject targets by operator manipulation, such as "whipping" or operating at a prescribed scanning speed, are virtually useless in prospecting. Under almost 100% of any circumstances your *sample* must be moved across the face of a searchcoil in a controlled manner to assure correct identification.

During the early days of metal detecting, much literature was produced (by these authors, too!) on prospecting with detectors. The majority of that writing revolved around the ancient, but trusty, workhorse of the industry, the beat frequency oscillator (BFO) metal detector. We old-timers can become almost romantic in recounting our successes with it. We loved that old detector, but the simple fact is that today the BFO is obsolete. It is no longer manufactured. Anyone who has been successful in the gold fields with a BFO has found this success magnified through use of a proper modern detector. Our experience conclusively proves the truth of that statement. The new universal computerized instruments with microprocessor controls perform even better in the gold fields, as in all other treasure hunting environments.

Bench Testing

Methodical bench testing enables the operator to learn more about a detector's capabilities before taking it into the gold fields. The following tests which should be performed with the searchcoil perpendicular to a bench, floor or other non-metallic surface are applicable to any gold-hunting detector. We're going to give precise instructions for bench testing Garrett's Scorpion Gold Stinger in both its Discriminate modes.

1. Rotate **Discrimination** control fully counterclockwise with **Master Control** switch set at *MOTION DISC.*

2. With the **Discrimination** control at the *0* position bring various gold and metallic targets across the bottom of the searchcoil at a distance of about two inches. Each target will cause the sound to increase. This is true nondiscriminating operation. You will also want to test various rocks and ore samples while in the this mode. When the **Discrimination** control is set at *0*, it is at the absolute tuning point between metal and mineral. Any sound from a target will indicate the presence of some conductive metal.

3. Rotate the control to the *3* or *4* position and the sound will decrease or cease when small nails are scanned across the bottom of the searchcoil. Test various objects at some of the higher discrimination settings and note the results.

Never rotate the **Discrimination** knob any farther clockwise than necessary to eliminate targets you do not wish to detect.

Odd-shaped samples should always be held in several different positions when testing. An elongated (football-shape) sample, for example, could give one reading if held broadside and a different reading if the pointed end faces the coil. Flat metallic samples produce larger detector signals when the flat side is parallel to the bottom of the searchcoil. On the other hand, iron mineral samples produce approximately the same negative signal, regardless of their orientation.

Always move the sample across your searchcoil. Reasonably rapid motions should produce speaker variations that can be heard easily.

Ground Balancing

Most serious gold hunters will use a detector that offers a Deepseeking all metal detection mode. In this mode it is necessary to make certain that your detector is ground balanced precisely. This will enable the instrument to ignore properly the ground minerals that are present, while detecting gold nuggets and other metallic objects. Such ground balancing can be automatic or manual.

Manual ground balancing also enables an operator to set ground balance slightly positive to find tiny nuggets more easily or slightly negative to help eliminate hot rocks.

Great progress has been made in recent years by the Garrett Engineering Lab and those of some other companies in the development of automatic ground balancing, a function known as *Ground Track*™ on Garrett's CX II and CX III models. These engineers have been so successful that a great many gold hunters today actually prefer to use detectors that offer a Deepseeking all metal mode with automatic ground balance. Although it is difficult for many veteran gold hunters to accept, manual ground balancing may soon become a "thing of the past."

Even so, you should know how to ground balance a detector properly in case you're using an instrument without the automatic feature or if you ever need to balance your instrument either slightly positive or slightly negative. We'll describe the procedures for ground balancing the Scorpion Gold Stinger. They will be similar on other quality detectors.

Press the **Master Control** switch to the left to activate the Deepseeking all metal (manual ground balancing) mode. In this mode the Stinger will respond with an increase in sound to the presence of any metal or conductive mineral target beneath its searchcoil. For maximum depth and best operation when prospecting or searching mineralized ground, always operate in the Deepseeking mode.

Iron mineralization can be balanced (canceled out) in this Deepseeking mode by use of the **Ground Balance** controls. To determine if adjustment is necessary, lower the searchcoil, stopping at a height of about two inches above the ground. Make sure no metallic targets are under the coil. When you lower the searchcoil, audio level will either increase, decrease or remain constant.

If the sound remains constant, the **Ground Balance** control is adjusted properly. If the audio level decreases, raise the searchcoil and rotate the **Ground Balance** control to the right (clockwise). Press the **Tune** button and release. Lower the searchcoil again. If the audio level now increases, the control has been adjusted too far. Raise the searchcoil and rotate the control back to the left (counterclockwise). Press the **Tune** button again and release. (Since **Ground Balance** is a 10-turn control, you should not be hesitant about turning it as much as necessary!)

Continue this "tuning" process until there is no change or only a slight change when the searchcoil is lowered to operating height. You will soon learn how to use this control in to achieve precise ground balance quickly. Remember to rotate the control **clockwise** when speaker sound *decreases* and **counterclockwise** when the sound *increases*. Also, remember that because the knob is a 10-turn control, it might occasionally be necessary for you to turn it several complete revolutions to achieve proper ground balance.

While using manual ground balance as you search in the Deepseeking all metal mode, you should occasionally raise the searchcoil, then lower it. If your audio level changes, readjust the ground balance according to the above instructions. Such readjustment will sometimes be necessary because of the changing concentrations of ground minerals, a condition that is fairly common when you are prospecting in gold country.

Adjustments for Sampling

Metal/mineral ore sample identification can be achieved in the Discriminate mode. Rotate your detector's discrimination control knob to its *0* setting, usually fully counterclockwise. Set GTA detectors in a mode with zero discrimination (*all* Lower Scale segments visible). At these settings properly calibrated discriminating instruments (*all* GTA and other Garrett detectors) will respond positively when *any* metallic object is passed across the bottom of its searchcoil. Even tiny nails, regardless of their orientation, should produce a positive speaker sound when passed across the center of the searchcoil. Remember, *all* metal objects *must* produce a positive indication. If this cannot be achieved, the discrimination control has not been correctly calibrated.

To sum up — if your detector has been correctly calibrated (calibration of *every* detector manufactured by Garrett is tested before it leaves the factory), you can check ore samples accurately in the Discriminate mode simply by setting your discrimination control at its zero setting.

Hot Rocks

A hot rock is simply a rock that contains a quantity and/or density of non-conductive iron mineral that responds as *metal* when the ground balance controls of your detector are adjusted to a particular setting.

To use a cliche and to use it aptly, these mineralized pebbles are the absolute bane of an electronic prospector's existence. There is no getting away from them if you are diligent and persistent in your search for gold. Furthermore, they can drive you crazy if you let them. Let us emphasize how vital it is that you learn to understand these little pests and to know how to respond to them properly.

When you are operating with your detector in the Deepseeking all metal mode, the signal you receive from a hot rock will be the same as you would receive from a metallic object. The signal is positive and unmistakably "metal." Of course, you should first try to identify any target before digging. The method used to identify hot rocks is explained fully in Chapter Nine. We mention the subject here because recognizing and identifying them is so important to anyone searching for gold with a metal detector.

Hot rocks can be found in jumbled rock piles as well as in areas that look as if they have never been disturbed. They contain no conductive material. Their iron mineral content, however, differs enough from that of surrounding rocks to disturb the delicate ground balance of your detector to such an extent that the hot rocks can present themselves as metal targets.

Hot rocks are "freaks" or "oddballs" of nature. They should not be where they are, and they should not cause your detector to react the way that it does. But, they do! Simply stated, however, hot rocks are "there," and all of us who search for gold must occasionally deal with them. With a properly calibrated detector you can identify them quickly, and they will become to you exactly what they are to veteran prospectors — tolerable pests.

Chapter 9

Metal•Mineral

Proper Identification...

T wo factors generally determine whether non-ferrous metals will produce a metallic signal when encountered by a metal detector — the quantity of metal that is present and the physical state in which it is found.

When the electromagnetic field of a metal detector's searchcoil is disturbed by a sufficient quantity of gold, silver, copper or other valued non-ferrous metals, the detector signals a metallic response — provided the metals are in a conductive state. Since some extremely rich ores are in sulfides, tellurides and other compounds that are not conductive, they do not produce a metallic response, regardless of their quantity or purity. Free milling ores of non-ferrous metals, however, generally produce good responses when the ores are encountered in sufficient quantities by a metal detector.

About the only mineral that a metal detector can recognize as "mineral," is magnetic black sand or magnetic iron (Fe_3O_4). A detector tuned in a true calibrated discriminate mode can easily determine whether the ore contains a predominance either of metal or of mineral. If the ore specimen contains neither metal nor mineral, the detector will produce no indication.

A "mineral" response from the detector does not necessarily indicate there is no metal present; rather, that there is a predominance of mineral. When the specimen signals a metallic response, you can be certain that it contains metal in conductive form in such quantities that you should investigate the specimen thoroughly. Such response capabilities of a modern detector with discrimination capability make it today's most important field tool for the identification of metal vs. mineral.

Make Your Own Samples

To understand how a metal detector signals the presence of metal, you should make your own "ore" samples. An older U.S. penny made of copper provides one of the metal samples you will need.

Producing your mineral sample will require a little more effort. Place a large iron nail or a piece of soft iron into a vise and file the nail with a very fine file. Place a piece of paper under the vise to collect the filings. The amount of filings required is about equal to the weight of a silver dime. Place these iron filings into a small plastic container (a medicine pill bottle is satisfactory) with a diameter about equal to that of a dime. Put enough glue in the bottle to cover your filings and let it solidify.

You have now produced a sample of non-conductive iron mineral that will cause a response from your metal detector identical to that which is caused by much of the iron mineral you find while prospecting. Remember that you will need a very fine-toothed file to make your filings of almost powder consistency. Leave the glued filings in the bottle.

Your next sample will demonstrate the difficulty of detecting silver oxides, gold dust and wire gold. Reduce a copper penny completely to filings as you did with the nail. Place these particles in the same size bottle as your iron filings and again pour in enough glue to hold them permanently. You now have what is basically an ore sample. It is composed of marginally conductive, non-ferrous ore whose presence in the electromagnetic field of your metal detector will cause the instrument to produce a "questionable" positive response.

Scan these samples with your detector. Study carefully the responses generated by each. Such practice will greatly aid your analysis of veins and pockets when you encounter them in the field, and you will begin to learn how to identify correctly the metal/mineral content of ore samples. Try to obtain samples of as many of the other ores mentioned in this book as possible.

Identifying Hot Rocks

The subject of hot rocks arises any time you must ground balance your detector properly to compensate for the mineral content of the soil over which you are searching. This subject is covered quite clearly in Chapter Eight. And, as that chapter notes, this happens quite frequently in gold country.

First of all, let us state firmly that this subject is not as important (or, complicated) as many beginning gold-seekers seem to think. To put it another way...hot rocks are generally not nearly the problem that some metal detector enthusiasts expect them to be. Or, as Roy once confided to Charles, "Skipper, I'm sorry we ever talked about the darned things. Hardly anyone paid much attention to hot rocks until we wrote about them!"

Yes, we were the ones who first began discussing (in print, at least) the stumbling block that hot rocks can present to someone hunting for gold with a metal detector. And, our comments apparently had an impact...judging from the correspondence we receive and the people with whom we talk. We seem to have magnified the importance of hot rocks and made them a real bugaboo for many hobbyists hunting gold with a metal detector.

And, you *should* be concerned about them. You don't want a hot rock to cause you to overlook a piece of gold ore, yet you don't want to misidentify a hot rock as precious metal. It's much the same as the early miners who filled their pokes so often with pyrite that it became known as "fool's gold."

After we identified the problem, however, some hobbyists became obsessed with the subject of hot rocks, sometimes to the extent that they seem to look for *them* rather than gold!

So, let's try to take the mystique out of the subject. Roy may be right; perhaps we never should have talked about hot rocks. But, since we did and since they are a fact of life, let's discuss them realistically.

Hot rocks (and hot spots) are simply isolated or "out-of-place" minerals that you occasionally encounter. Naturally, your detector hasn't been ground balanced for them since it's properly adjusted for the ground over which you are searching. Then, whenever you encounter any rocks (or soil) with a decidedly different mineral content, your detector will, of course, give a positive metallic signal. Believe me, this does not happen nearly so often as many neophyte electronic prospectors fear!

We have heard of some so-called "experts" who advise that you should actually grand balance your detector over a hot rock until it no longer sounds off, but this method is obviously self-defeating. If you're ground balanced for the hot rock, you'll be out of ground balance for the surrounding soil. Even if you should find several hot rocks together, don't ever ground balance your detector over them. You want it balanced for the ground over which you are scanning.

Let us reemphasize here, however, the importance of using a detector that has been properly designed and calibrated by its manufacturer for universal use, including prospecting. All metal detectors are *not suitable for prospecting*, despite claims that may be made for them — by the manufacturer or by anyone else.

The procedure for identifying mineral hot spots (and hot rocks) is a simple one, but it will require practice from you. To check to see if the "metal" response your detector has given comes from metal or mineral...first, pinpoint your target with the detector in the Deepseeking all metal mode and isolate it. Then, move the searchcoil to one side, lower it slightly or set it on the ground and switch to the Discriminate mode of operation. The Discrimination controls should be set to zero or to the level specified by the manufacturer as the calibrated level for ore sampling.

Now, with a constant sound (threshold) coming from your detector, pass the searchcoil back over the target you have isolated. Keep the searchcoil at the same distance from the ground, as just discussed. Maintaining constant searchcoil height may be difficult at first, but you can accomplish it with practice. If the sound level decreases (or goes silent), your target is magnetic iron ore or oxides. These are the *only* substances that will cause the signal to stop. When this happens, ignore the target, switch back into your Deepseeking mode and continue searching.

You have just exposed a *hot rock* or a piece of extremely rusted iron!

If, in the Discriminate mode your signal increases or remains steady, the target should be dug and investigated. Increase your variable discrimination control (usually by turning the knob clockwise) in steps and check the target at each setting by passing it across the bottom of your coil at a distance of about two inches. This will let you determine the amount of conductivity in this target. If you have previously practiced with your samples at varying discrimination levels, you already know the approximate point on the control where worthless specimens will be rejected. If you continue to receive a positive response after you have passed this setting, it is very possible that you have discovered a piece of conductive ore or a non-ferrous pocket.

You may have just *struck it rich!*

Chapter 10

Gold Nuggets
What Most Hobbyists Seek...

This term "nugget-hunting" is so ambiguous that no description of it could ever be complete. And, there are certainly no rules to follow or short cuts you can take. But, the fact of the matter is...that's what this book is really all about — nugget hunting. A gold nugget, whether it be the size of a pinhead or your fist, is what you're probably seeking when you go into the gold fields with a metal detector. This is especially true if you are relatively inexperienced in the hobby. It's the hope of finding nuggets that causes you to work so hard in learning to get the most from your metal detector. It's what brings you into the field. It's what this hobby of gold-hunting is all about!

This chapter will concern itself simply with basic instructions for finding nuggets in such various locations as streams, dry washes, old diggings and dredge piles. Never forget that hunting for gold is an outdoor activity. So, prepare yourself for an all-day search with appropriate clothing, food and water. Make certain you have the right kind of detector and that it is ground balanced properly (see Page 75). Check the ground balance from time to time because you might find it changing as mineral conditions beneath your searchcoil vary. We also recommend that you use headphones, especially when searching in or near noisy running water.

Always remember that gold is where you find it. But, you're much better off looking where nuggets have already been found. Talk to other gold-hunters and learn about their experiences. Sure, nobody is going to tell you exactly where to find a nugget. I know that we aren't! Why, if one of us knew exactly, he'd go get it himself! But, hobbyists love to boast of their discoveries and you can learn from them.

So, that's where you start hunting...where others have had success. Yet, when you're nugget hunting, remember that nuggets have been found in the most improbable places...in open desert areas with no mountains nearby, no apparent streambeds or placer deposits. We urge you, too, not to think like a human being. After all, it was nature that placed the nuggets where they are, not man. And, nature is random with few straight lines or right angles. For ourselves, then, we try to hunt *with* nature. We hunt in washes, eroded areas or channels cut into the ground. It's here that nature has eliminated some of the overburden to let your detector get closer to nuggets.

Dry Washes and Diggings

In wide wash areas with a thick layer of sand, we search close to the edges where nuggets might have become dislodged recently. But, in narrow channels we suggest that you search the entire wash...up the sides of both embankments.

In old streambeds and washes, look for obstructions that could have trapped nuggets. These can be rocks, tree roots and the like.

These nuggets, found with a detector ground balanced in a Deepseeking all metal mode, might have eluded a discriminating instrument

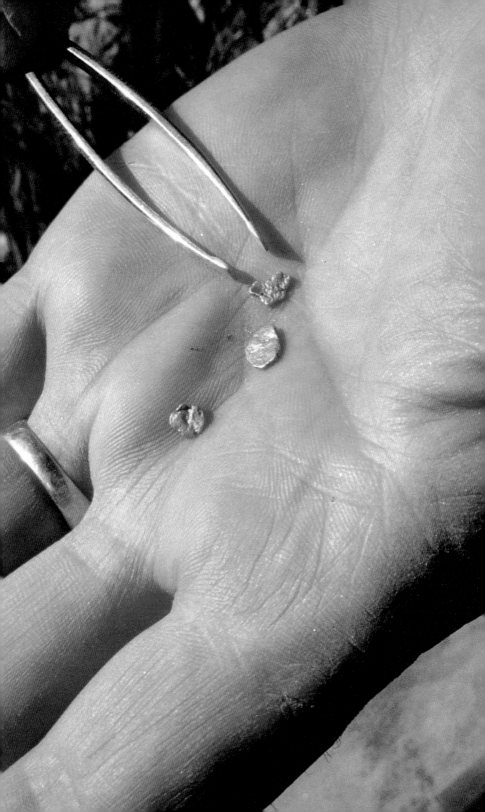

We recommend you not use a shovel in your actual digging for nuggets. Digging will go much quicker, especially in hard-packed soil, when you use another kind of tool. We suggest a medium-weight, rugged, short-handled mattock with a flat blade on one side and raking tines on the other. It should have a magnet embedded in the end of its handle. You'll notice Roy Lagal carrying such a tool in the photograph on the back cover, and Charles Garrett is using one in the photo on the facing page. Such tools are easily accessible at detector shops in gold-hunting areas or in mining supply stores.

When you're scanning be sure to overlap at least 50%, especially if you're seeking deep nuggets. Remember that the pattern of your signal becomes narrower the deeper it penetrates.

Caution: Searchcoil operating height will be determined by the amount of mineralization present and the size of rocks lying on the surface. You want your coil as close to the ground as possible, but you do *not* want to listen to any "chatter" from the jumbled mess of mineralized material that you are scanning over. There's always a danger that such chatter might cause you to overlook the true signals of conductive metals that your detector will transmit to you. Operating heights of even greater than two inches may be required in highly mineralized ground.

When we get a signal, we first pinpoint the target. Then, we swing our tool so that the blade strikes the ground ahead of it. That way, we won't damage any nugget or coin that we've discovered, and we rake the soil carefully with the tines of our tool to uncover this target.

Alerted to the possibility of nuggets by his detector, Charles Garrett uses a mattock to scrape material into a Gravity Trap gold pan for dry panning.

Train yourself to observe closely where you're digging. We've hunted with people who would be digging away when their target was lying exposed only a few inches away. If you can't locate the target visually, scan again with your detector, and you'll now get a louder signal because raking the soil away has placed you closer to your target. We recommend that you always carefully examine everything you find. Certainly, if you don't take time in the field, save all your finds for later examination. You can then discard your trash properly. You don't want to leave junk in the field for others to find. Why, you might be back yourself!

Begin searching with a general purpose 8 to 10-inch searchcoil. You're probably very familiar with it and you get relatively broad and deep coverage. After you've found a nugget or two with the general purpose searchcoil, you can switch...to a larger coil to locate deeper and, perhaps, larger nuggets...or, switch to the smaller Super Sniper 4 1/2-inch coil to intensify your search over the areas of discovery.

In fact, whenever you find a nugget, work the area to death. Search in a large radius around where you made your discovery. You know that one nugget was there. There could be others. And, never assume that just because an area has been worked by others that all its nuggets have been found. Remember, *you* haven't searched the area with *your* detector.

When you hear about an area where only shallow nuggets were found, always consider that the area wasn't worked properly or wasn't worked with a good, modern detector. When searching such a location, slow down and concentrate your search. The deep nuggets just might be there!

Don't necessarily avoid areas where there are obviously a lot of junk metal items. Such areas have often not been searched properly just because people didn't want to have to dig this junk. So, go the "extra mile" and search junky areas. Either dig all targets or use a little discrimination judiciously. We know specific instances where individuals persisted in such areas and found large nuggets.

You're going to find some trash. In gold country the most common trash seems to be nails and eyelets from shoes and boots as well as buttons, hooks and other fasteners from clothing. Concerning trash, here's where your magnet speeds up your search. When you detect a target you can't find, rub the magnet end of your mattock in the dirt you have raked. If you've found a bit of iron trash, it will stick to the magnet. If nothing sticks to the magnet, re-scan the hole carefully before you move on.

Concerning discrimination, remember that pure gold is rarely found in nature. All gold nuggets are some sort of alloy. Thus, any discrimination you use might eliminate some of these alloy metals from detection, making nuggets even harder to find. Long-time detector enthusiasts recommend no discrimination when searching for nuggets.

Hunting In Water

Make certain that you are using a submersible searchcoil and scan about four inches or higher above the bottom of the stream, moving slowly over your search area. Operating height will depend upon mineralization of the area and the amount of "chatter" these minerals are causing you to hear.

A plastic gold pan and a good shovel will improve your ability to recover gold nuggets in a stream, as well as a pry bar to loosen compacted rocks and gravel.

When you discover a metallic target, scoop it up along with the surrounding sand and gravel and place it in your plastic gold pan. Test the entire pan of material with your detector to determine if you have recovered the target that produced the original signal. If the target is not in the pan, dump its contents back into the water, locate your target again with the detector and scoop up another shovel of material from the stream bed into your pan. Continue repeating this process until you have your target in the pan. Even then, recheck the streambed where you scooped up the material for additional targets.

When you are certain that you have the metallic target in your gold pan, first try to locate it visually by carefully sorting and discarding the rocks and pieces of gravel. If you cannot spot a gold nugget, further concentrate the material by panning.

Remember that floods can carry a stream outside its banks and leave behind nuggets far out of the normal watercourse. This could have happened many times over the centuries. Always be on the lookout for "traps" on the banks of streams where such nuggets might have collected. These can sometimes be found by looking for pools that are not associated with the flowing stream.

In those streambeds that were hydraulically mined you should be able to find large areas of exposed bedrock. Even if these were totally cleaned out by the original miners (which they probably were not!) new deposits might have been made since.

This business of "new deposits" is something that you should always remember, especially when you are told that an area has been "cleaned out years ago." The normal flow of a stream, as well as flash floods and winds, will continually bring new deposits to a location. In addition, those detectors that "cleaned out" an area so many years ago most likely did not have the sensitivity or the gold-finding capabilities of the modern detector that you are using. If you're using any Garrett CX or a Scorpion Gold Stinger detector, you can take our word for it!

Dredge Pile Searching

The method of detection described above can be used on old dredge tailings either in the water or on banks of streams. Practically all rock piles present on banks alongside streams are dredge tailings. Old dredge tailings have produced some fantastic gold finds for treasure hunters with metal detectors. Never overlook these opportunities!

In their efforts to recover precious metal, prospectors came into gold country with huge earth-moving devices and scooped out streams down to bedrock, literally turning the land inside out. Countless tons of rock were removed in a relentless search for gold. Since gold is one of nature's heavier elements, the actions of wind and water work with gravity to pull it down to the lowest possible level. This is especially true in stream beds where the gold finally reaches bedrock. There it may lie for eons, awaiting the prospector...whether he has a huge dredge or a sophisticated modern metal detector.

Prospectors with dredges scooped up vast quantities of rocks which they immediately began processing, first by classifying according to size. This is done with a trommel, the sieve-like device that sizes materials as they are scooped from the streambed. What is left in the dredge piles depends on the size of the holes in the trommel. Huge conveyor belts transported waste material and large rocks to locations on the banks of the stream where they lie today, often in unsightly heaps.

These are the dredge piles that have been successfully searched by so many electronic prospectors. Not all of the materials in these piles is worthless. Occasionally, large nuggets escaped the eyes of the dredgers and their sorting equipment and went into the dredge piles. Small nuggets passed through in mud balls. They are still there awaiting your detector.

Scan these piles as you would scan any other location. When you get a signal, carefully scoop up as much of the material around the signal as possible in a plastic gold pan. Then, scan the material in the pan to find out what caused the signal. Make certain your detector is precisely ground balanced, and listen closely with headphones for increases in sound. It is necessary to use a pan because whatever you detect in a dredge pile can easily fall down into the pile as you dig for it. Of course, you'll have to use a plastic pan because you could learn nothing from scanning a metal pan.

Remember that dredge piles are simply piles of individual rocks that were tumbled from many different locations...first by nature and later by the dredgers. It's possible to dig down into the pile to expose your searchcoil to a different layer of material, but it's time-consuming. Too, it's quite a chore to lower the scanning surface over even a small area.

A good detector with precise ground balancing and calibrated discrimination will amaze you with the number of things it enables you to recover from the desert. Despite the advertising claims that you will read, there are only a few such detectors. We can speak from experience about the capabilities of Garrett's Scorpion Gold Stinger and its entire line-up of CX detectors.

Some additional thoughts on nugget hunting:

– Keep your eyes open; there will occasionally be nuggets on the surface.

– A good time to search visually is right after a rain, especially in bright sunlight. The rain has washed away loose soil and helped expose nuggets on the surface or those just below it.

– In rocky areas move aside as many rocks as possible so that you can scan under them. Scan closely around all those rocks too large to move.

– Physical recovery of nuggets from dry sand can be accomplished with a plastic gold pan in the same manner you retrieved targets from a stream. In fact, the process should be somewhat easier without water rushing around you and your feet slipping on wet rocks!

– Keep a map showing where you have found nuggets. A pattern might develop and you may want to scan again over the places where nuggets were found.

– Always remain confident that your modern detector is doing a good job for you. It will penetrate iron mineral soil to detect nuggets. And, it will never "lie" to you. It's up to you to interpret its signals. And, you can learn this through practice, practice, practice.

Chapter 11

Old Mines

Searching with a Detector...

hen you find an old mine that you consider a likely source of gold, begin by checking its floor with your metal detector. There is always the remote possibility that you are the first person who has looked here since the mine was abandoned, and you can occasionally find high grade ore in older mine tunnels and shafts. Remember that they were worked by less modern methods than you are using.

Few weekend miners seem to realize that tunnel floors of old mines can be some of the most productive areas for searching with a modern metal detector. *All* of the ore that left that mine crossed the tunnel floor at least one time. Some pieces of valuable ore almost certainly fell from carts. It is likely that all fallen ore was not recovered but eventually became covered with rock and other debris. This high grade ore has lain there unnoticed for decades, just waiting for some lucky hobbyist to find it.

Begin your mine search by ground balancing your metal detector (see Page 75) to cancel out ground mineralization. Make a general sweep of the tunnel floor, collecting all samples that give a metal reading. Remember, though, that there are likely to be many small iron objects in an old mine — rail spikes, pieces of the rail itself and hangers for candles and mining lamps. Spikes that were sometimes used to secure the tunnel shoring will be picked up by your metal detector. If rails are still in place, you can work closer to them by using smaller searchcoils.

Once you have collected a number of likely looking ore samples, lay your metal detector flat as you did for bench testing. Test each of your rock samples individually. Continue this testing as you work the tunnel thoroughly from one end to the other. Use a mattock or rock pick to dig beneath the surface debris to locate all likely looking samples to test.

Here's an additional tip on this type of mine searching: The "pay streak" will normally always contain a much higher metal or mineral content than the ordinary rock of the tunnel. For this reason save *any* unusual samples for later careful examination.

Ore Pockets and Veins

Many of the old miners missed pockets and veins of high grade ore. Because of the limitations of their equipment, they may have passed within inches of the gold and silver that they sought as they chewed into the mountainside in their search for new deposits. Modern metal detectors can easily pinpoint these valuable pockets and veins for the electronic prospector.

Since you will find most mine tunnels driven through highly mineralized or magnetic material, your detector must be ground balanced as precisely as possible to cancel the effects of these minerals. We also recommend that you always adjust your audio so that you maintain a faint but constant sound from the speaker. (Of course, headphones are always better!)

Operate your searchcoil approximately four to twelve inches from the tunnel wall, depending upon the amount of iron mineralization present. Scan the walls and ceiling carefully, marking or taking note of any positive (metallic) signals. Ore containing a sufficient amount of conductivity will respond positively as metal.

Ground balancing your detector to compensate for a mineral background will cause it to give a metal response also to hot rocks and certain iron ore deposits. This occurs simply because your detector has not been ground balanced for these iron elements. Identification of hot rocks and hot spots (see Pages 82-3) is no problem whatsoever to a modern, properly calibrated detector.

Searching inside mines definitely requires a detector with two circuits — one to locate the target and a properly calibrated discriminating metal-mineral circuit to identify it. Many detectors do not include these calibrated circuits that tell you if you have found a conductive element or worthless iron ore.

We reemphasize the importance of both proper design and proper calibration of a detector by its manufacturer for universal use, including prospecting. We repeat that *all* metal detectors are *not* suitable for prospecting, despite claims made for them. We regularly hear about hobbyists who take the "wrong" detector into the gold fields and then declare to their friends, "You can't find gold with a metal detector." They certainly couldn't...because they were using the wrong type of detector!

Remember that iron pyrites have a much *lower* (poorer) conductivity factor than non-ferrous ore. Pyrites will be rejected by the discriminate circuitry while the detector still accepts low grade non-ferrous ores. Keep in mind that all ore bodies may not necessarily be solid metal, and your response may be rather faint unless the ore is of extremely high conductivity. Remember your homemade non-ferrous ore sample, and don't overlook weak signals. Detecting non-ferrous or ore that is either non-conductive or has low conductivity can be very difficult. Of course, the ore content must still be determined by analysis or assay, but this important detection capability of prospecting instruments is largely overlooked, even by professional miners and geologists.

Elsewhere in this book we describe the method for analyzing detectable substances using your detector in its

Discriminate mode. Remember, that while conductive analysis is possible in the Discriminate mode, only chemical assays can be relied upon to produce qualitative and quantitative data.

To those of you who have worked in mines with BFO detectors, we urge that you return with a modern ground-balanced instrument — especially, if you considered your search successful. Those "negative" BFO readings you ignored may contain much more than magnetic iron!

Words of Caution

Always remember these warnings:
– Abandoned mines can be very dangerous.
– Never work alone around a mine.

When you are exploring or working around deserted mine shafts and tunnels, extreme caution should always be exercised. You can be certain that shoring timbers have rotted somewhat over the years, and water seepage may have loosened once-solid tunnel walls. Any loud noise or impact against the timbers or walls of a tunnel could bring a mountain down on the old mine.

Equal care should be used any time you even peer down an old mine shaft. Not only is there a chance the earth at its edge could crumble, causing you to loose your footing, but poisonous fumes coming from shafts have been known to kill people. And, they weren't even prospectors, just tourists who wanted to look down an old mine!

Never let all members of your party enter a mine at the same time. Someone should always remain at the surface or at the entrance to a mine to summon help, if needed.

Don't forget the laws of ownership. Just because an old mine *looks* deserted, you do not necessarily have the right to enter, much less begin searching with a detector. There is probably somebody with a valid claim to that mine, and he or she might object to your doing a little high grading on their property. Some old timers object violently...and they show it! Remember, it is always best and proper to gain permission to search. Very few claim holders will object to your electronic prospecting, particularly if you offer to give them helpful information on any veins or mineral pockets you might locate.

Old Mine Dumps

As you travel through the deserted gold fields, you will observe many abandoned tunnels, rock heaps (tailings) and piles of ore that never made it to the stamp mill to be crushed. By using your metal detector properly to test these rocks, you can often recover many good ore samples and an occasional gold nugget.

When you search for high grade ore in a mine dump, remember that during the working life of the mine, a tremendous amount of rocks and other debris from shafts and tunnels may have been deposited in that dump. Only a small portion of it may consist of tailings from the vein itself. Thus, you can readily see how important it is to take rock and ore samples from many different locations, especially from the top of the dump.

To check for high grade ore samples lay your detector flat and tune it precisely (just as you did for bench testing). Then, move your selected samples, one at a time, across the center of the searchcoil to test for metal. After a reasonable number of samples from one location have been tested and no metal has been located, move to another area of the dump. If, after prolonged testing, you do not recover at least a few metallic specimens, it may be that the ore was of very low grade composition and was never of any great value.

Do not overlook the possibilities of working these old ore dumps. Old time miners worked hard for hundreds of hours to bring these rocks from beneath the earth. Many beautiful silver and gold specimens of considerable value have been found this way...hiding inside worthless-looking chunks of mine tailing debris.

You can scan over rock piles, but in most cases it is difficult to ground balance a detector for this. Since each rock may contain a different amount of iron, just a slight movement of the searchcoil can result in a significant change in the minerals beneath it. This can result in rapid and pronounced ground "unbalance" of the detector. Also, there may be many hot rocks present in the dump.

We urge you to try it anyway! Choose a spot where you are able to ground balance your detector adequately; then, scan several inches above the rocks rather than close to the surface.

A possibility for mines that you encounter on hillsides is to scan the ground area below the mine entrance itself. Float from the veins might have washed away for years, even before the mine itself was dug. With the right detector you can find this float on the hillsides below the mine.

While prospecting with metal detectors in Chihuahua, Mexico, we located three veins of silver that had been totally overlooked by early day miners. In scanning the walls of a mine owned by Javier Castellanos, Charles received three readings that demanded further investigation. Two of the readings proved to be silver pockets, and the third was a vein of native silver approximately one-half an inch in width. As Javier tooled his way into the mine wall, this newly discovered vein grew larger as it continued below floor level and proved to be one foot wide! This silver vein and the pockets perhaps would have been lost forever if the electronic metal detector had not signaled their presence.

Don't overlook the abundance of ore that is always to be found lying around on the tunnel floors or beside rails between the mine and mill or loading area. By testing these ore samples with a detector you can uncover valuable specimens overlooked by the original miners. No matter where the ore came from in a mine, when it fell off a cart, it was often not considered valuable enough to recover — because it contained no gold that was visible to the naked eye, the only gold-seeking tool possessed by early-day miners.

Chapter 12

field Prospecting
Other Ways to Find Gold...

The title of this chapter, or "field searching" as it is
sometimes called, could cover the entire spec-
trum of recreational prospecting. It encompasses
a wide variety of searching for precious metal,
such as locating deep veins, looking for placer or
nugget deposits, hunting for rich float material and
pocket hunting. Previous chapters have given suggestions concerning some of these types of hunting.

You should search for gold in areas where it has been
found. Always remember that volumes of geologic and
engineering data have been accumulated concerning
most major geographic areas where large discoveries of
precious metals have been made. We urge you to conduct research and to make use of as much of this material
as you can. Technical manuals detailing these discoveries, however, are written by mining engineers, professional prospectors and others in the mining field, many
of whom — despite their expertise — are not familiar
with modern metal detectors. Our suggestions in this
book may sound simplistic, yet they pertain specifically
to searching for gold with a modern metal detector and
include procedures used today by the most successful
electronic prospectors.

Field prospecting is where you'll be using all of the
knowledge that you have gained previously in practicing

with your detector and in your bench tests as well as your other outdoor experiences.

Grid Patterns

Searching in grid patterns is a method that has proved successful in field prospecting when looking for veins. It offers the opportunity of approaching a vein or other type deposit from two different directions, avoiding the distinct possibility of walking parallel to a vein but never actually crossing it. Set up a fixed grid or crisscross pattern and sweep your largest searchcoil across it evenly.

Always adjust your detector in the Deepseeking all metal mode, balanced to the mineralization of the surrounding ground (see Page 75). If available on your detector, manual tuning is preferred. Walk slowly in as straight a line as topography permits, scanning a wide path with the searchcoil ahead of you. When you reach the end of one of your "lines," turn and walk a parallel path in the opposite direction approximately 10 feet from the first path. Continue until you have covered the area selected. Then, repeat this procedure, except walk parallel paths at 90-degree angles to the first set of paths. Now, you have completed your fixed grid or crisscross pattern search of the area.

If your detector sound increases and/or the LCD or meter pointer shows any increase while you are scanning, notice the intensity and the duration of the increase. You may have discovered a vein or ore pocket.

On the other hand, your detector may have changed its tuning due to atmospheric conditions, interference, bumping of controls, etc. Do not touch your detector's controls. Rather, scan back to that point where you first noticed an increase. If the speaker and/or meter decreases to the previous level, your detector's positive response was caused by conditions in the ground, not some detector or operator problem.

Turn around and scan the same path. As you reach the point where the sound changed earlier, it should again change if you are detecting an ore vein or pocket.

As you continue walking, pay close attention to the detector's audio responses. They should either increase further or drop off to your initial tuning level. If responses are "increasing," your ore is getting richer, or it is lying closer to the surface. When the responses return to your initial tuning level, you have walked over or past the ore deposit. Plot or map the deposits or veins. If there are several, note where they cross or crisscross each other beneath the surface.

After you have found detectable ore deposits, try to identify their nature by operating your detector in the Discriminate mode. In this mode the detector will indicate whether your deposit is predominantly iron (nonconductive pyrites) or predominantly non-ferrous material. Veins crisscross each other beneath the surface, and a vein of gold may be bisected by several iron veins. Location of these veins can be plotted fairly accurately by paying careful attention to the responses from your detector. You will also receive positive metallic indications from heavy concentrates (pockets) of magnetic black sand. Since such pockets often contain gold, they should always be investigated. Refer to the forthcoming discussion on mapping veins/ore deposits.

Ore Veins

Contrary to what you may believe, large mining companies do not conduct nearly the amount of field prospecting that many amateur prospectors imagine. Profit is the reason. A large corporation spends its time in efforts that directly result in profits. Since prospecting takes a great deal of time with no guarantee of profit, the big companies rely to a large extent on individual prospectors to make finds that they can exploit.

It's only a remote possibility but if you should be fortunate enough to locate a rich ore vein or deposit, it might prove of value to one of the large mining corporations. The recreational miner who enjoys just being in the wilderness for a relaxing weekend or vacation, whether gold is found or not, is more apt to seek out the difficult gold deposits than are the large companies. Searching for gold will take you into some of the most beautiful areas of our great country. It will offer you the opportunity to camp in fantastic natural settings. Yet, your efforts might result in that once-in-a-lifetime chance for "the really big one." Plus, it's nice to fantasize!

All types of gold deposits are believed to have originated as an ore vein formed during the volcanic activity of past eons, and such veins may go deep into a mountain and be fabulously rich. When such a lode is located, mining companies will literally jump at the opportunity to purchase rights to extract ore from this vein and smelt it into pure metal.

Deep Pockets and Veins

Deep veins are usually a composition of several metals and minerals. Thus, vigilance must be exercised because signals from a deep vein may sound very faint even through your headphones and especially from your detector's speaker. Evaluate all signals by considering vein magnitude, the direction in which the vein appears to lie and how far it extends beneath the surface.

In seeking deep veins use the largest coil with which your detector is equipped. Pay close attention to all responses. Investigation of irregular or unusual signals will many times lead you to pay dirt.

Over

Authors take advantage of the work of heavy equipment which has exposed rocks that might contain nuggets or ore samples.

Facing

Good finds have been made in rock piles such as Charles Garrett is searching here, which were left behind after dredges had cleaned out streams.

The Depth Multiplier

In seeking large and deep veins you may want to use the Depth Multiplier two-box searchcoil which enables a compatible detector to search four to eight times deeper for large targets. It's easy to use the Depth Multiplier attachment. Just get into a basic Deepseeking mode, and it is not necessary to ground balance the detector. Wear headphones and set your audio threshold for faint sound. Be sure you aren't carrying a large metal object such as a shovel or large knife even though a few coins in your pocket may not matter. Hold the detector and fully extend your arm. Let the detector cradle in your fingers as Charles Garrett is doing in the photo on the back cover.

Slowly walk across the area you wish to search. Listen carefully for an increase in the audio level. When you hear the louder sound, stop and scratch a mark on the ground with your shoe. Continue walking without adjusting any of the detector's controls. When you have walked across the object you have just detected, the audio will return to its threshold level. Walk a few more feet before turning around and walking a return path. At the point where the audio increases as you are walking from this direction, make another mark on the ground. Your target will lie at the center point between your two marks on the ground.

Over

A 12-inch searchcoil is used to enable a detector to look behind the walls of an old mine to seek veins that early-day miners might have missed.

Facing

Charles Garrett and Bob Podhrasky exercise safety precautions that must always be taken when searching old mines.

Searching for and finding surface "float," or large chunks of ore, is an interesting aspect of prospecting. Use large searchcoils or the Depth Multiplier when searching for float. Then, when you have located a target, work in a grid pattern. Set the detector's tuning to enable you to hear continuously a slightly audible threshold sound and make wide side-to-side sweeps with your searchcoil. Because the response area may be quite wide, you should cover enough area in your sweep to be able to determine the edges (start and finish) of the signal. Within reason, the amount of response from your detector's signal should permit you to judge the depth of the vein.

When using the Depth Multiplier to search for float, follow the instructions given previously in this chapter.

Mapping Vein/Ore Deposits

Once you have detected an ore deposit, you will want to know whether you have discovered an isolated pocket only a few feet in diameter or an intricate network of iron and non-ferrous veins that cross and crisscross each other. You will find that mapping your newly found deposit is both challenging and intriguing. One reminder before you start mapping: make certain your detector is precisely ground balanced for mineralization in the area you seek to map.

Follow the grid-pattern searching techniques described earlier in this chapter, paying careful attention to detector responses as you plot them on paper. Responses by your detector from the veins below will vary widely, according to the width of the veins and/or how the iron oxides have leached out into the surrounding earth matrix. It is possible that a vein only one foot wide can leach out such an area that it appears several feet wide to your detector.

You may find that your detector response will increase and remain at this greater level for some scan distance before returning to your previous level. On the other hand, detector responses may change quite often, indicating the possibility of a network of veins. Carefully evaluate those areas you are scanning when your detector's responses change several times. While field searching, regularly check both the ground balance of your detector and its threshold level. Pay close attention to the detector's responses as you walk atop the vein or deposit. Try to determine not just if the detector responses change but also how much they change. Variations can indicate several magnetic ore pockets or perhaps contact points where veins bisect ore deposits or other veins.

In areas that have previously been worked by prospectors, careful detector readings can many times tell an experienced hobbyist of an extremely rich pocket or the place where a rich vein has "slipped" and become "lost" from known pockets and veins. The veteran detector operator will generally be able to correctly identify all deposits found by his or her instrument. Of course, core drilling to obtain samples for assaying is the easiest (and, sometimes, the only) way to determine the ultimate value of a discovery.

Placer Deposits

Placer mining is a most popular type of recreational prospecting. It offers the amateur miner a greater chance of recovering gold at very little equipment expense since less equipment is required than in other types of prospecting. In addition, such vicarious pleasures as the enjoyment of nature and healthy outdoor exercise seldom let placer mining become a chore. It is always a pleasure!

Even as you read this, your chances for placer mining success are getting better as rock deposits in gold country are eroded by wind, water and normal earth movements. These actions of nature release precious gold from the veritable prison of rock in which it has been held captive for centuries. As the heavier gold seeks lower levels, runoff from rain and melting snow move it down mountain slopes into freshets and brooks which carry it into larger streams. During periods of water movement, streams in the gold fields are heavy with dirt, rock, other debris and...*gold*. As gravity carries everything along, heavier materials — which includes gold — become trapped along the way as they sink below the lighter dirt and rocks which are being swept downstream.

Nature offers placer gold countless millions of opportunities for entrapment. Because it is heavier than the other materials with which it is flowing, gold is pulled by gravity to the lowest possible level wherever it is found. Gold, therefore, lodges in hollow depressions, cracks and crevices in the bedrock of any waterway in which it is being carried. Tiny bits of the golden metal also become entangled in tree and grass roots and sink in the backwaters behind large boulders. The successful placer miner will soon learn to spot these traps and check them out with metal detector and gold pan.

Because fast-moving water has already done part of the work of sifting and sorting among rocks, gravel and gold, placer mining (panning) in streams is easier than dry panning. Of course, any type of panning is easier than hard rock mining which requires large amounts of equipment, plus the actual effort required to move tons of rock to recover gold. This is why most recreational miners try to sell to large companies any hard rock claims they might discover. It is much easier and more pleasant for the recreational miner to spend limited prospecting time in "working" with the more enjoyable opportunities of placer mining.

Dry Washes

Years of watching movies and television have given most people the idea that gold is found only in streams and rivers and only in deserted areas of the Western and Mountain States. Not so!

A piece of quartz weighing more than 17 pounds and heavily laden with gold was found with a Garrett detector in North Georgia just last year.

True, it is easier to recover gold if there is a good supply of running water, but water is never a necessity. The old-timers almost always followed the stream beds because they knew that if gold was there, it would be moved downstream by water from the mountains. And, early placer mining prospectors used this water to pan the heavier gold from sand and gravel because it was the easiest way to find it. Using today's modern gold pan, with its built-in riffle traps, a weekend prospector can find gold in a pan even without water.

What about the old dry washes? They were obviously once stream beds, and may be dangerous in flash floods. But, they have not contained water for any length of time, perhaps for centuries. Remember that these dry beds can contain gold, and that it became deposited in them just as it is now being deposited in streams of flowing water. Until the development of the modern metal detector, finding gold in dry areas presented the prospect of panning literally acres of dry ground. A discouraging proposition! With today's modern ground balanced metal detectors, prospecting is much easier, and the dry washes that were passed up during the last century can prove quite productive.

Productive also are old placer diggings. An early day placer miner would not have seen a large nugget unless it gleamed brightly. Remember, he had only his eyesight to use as a locating tool. Today's recreational miner can locate nuggets even though they are enclosed in rock or mud or buried under a layer of sand. By using the detector to scan the old diggings and placer mining areas, any gold that was simply bypassed can be found easily. In most instances, use of a correctly designed, quality metal detector is the only method by which these long-over-looked deposits can be found. In *all* instances, the use of a detector is the fastest, most practical way to pursue recreational mining. With a quality detector — designed for universal use like any of Garrett's Master Hunter CX detectors or, primarily for prospecting, the Scorpion Gold Stinger — you can cover in minutes or hours what took months and years for the old prospectors who were limited to their shovels and pans.

Pocket Hunting

You have already learned that "float" can be defined as ore that broke off somehow from the mother lode and was carried away (usually down hills) by gravity, wind, water, earth movement or other acts of nature. Float can be found lodged in hollow places and behind boulders and other barriers to its downhill movement. These heavy pieces of ore form pockets on hillsides and have often been covered by an overburden of rock and gravel that has washed in on top of the gold ore.

Modern ground-balanced detectors can locate these rich pockets of metallic ore. Large searchcoils are preferable because they can search deeper and cover more ground. Both attributes will prove advantageous and the Depth Multiplier should always be considered.

Begin your search for pockets and/or float on depressions in hillsides or in gullies, creek bottoms and other areas where you reason logically that heavy pieces of float might have stopped. Once you begin to locate float ore, work upstream or uphill from your initial discovery and try to locate the source. Remember that ore is a combination material and may not produce as strong a reading as a solid metallic object. Do not overlook faint signals. When you get a reading over a pile of rocks, lay down your detector and proceed to scan the rocks, *one at a time,* across the bottom of your searchcoil as you practiced in your bench tests. By following this procedure you can learn which rock(s) produced the signal.

Whether working in a creekbed or on a hillside, ground balance your detector carefully and sweep the searchcoil two to six inches above the surface, depending on the "chatter" you get from iron mineralization. Listen carefully for faint signals that can come from deep pockets or those that have only a low percentage of metal. (Some iron mineral may also be present.) Nevertheless, if the pocket is relatively rich (conductive) and not too deep, you will mostly likely get a pronounced positive (metallic) response from your detector.

Chapter 13

Rockhounds
Can Use Detectors Too...

A rockhound is defined by the government as "an amateur who hunts and collects rocks and minerals as a hobby." For such an individual a modern metal detector can be invaluable in helping locate and identify valuable samples.

Many veteran rockhounds will tell you that nothing can replace the knowledge gained by experience in identifying semi-precious stones and gems. And, they're right...to an extent.

Yet, what happens when the valuable specimen defies the naked eye — and other senses of smell, touch, taste and feel...when your specimen is somehow hidden within another rock? No eye can look inside a rock the way that a detector can. Such hidden specimens can be overlooked by even the most experienced collector.

The rockhound should consider the detector as standard equipment that can be used to locate and identify conductive metal specimens that defy the naked eye. Yet, like the rest of us, the rockhound must remember that although a detector can be a valuable tool — sometimes, the *most* valuable one — it is only a tool and nothing more. It must be used properly and in the right places.

To maximize a detector's value a rockhound must learn all about this instrument and what it can accomplish. Thus, we urge them to become familiar with modern metal detectors. If you haven't looked at one in a few years, you'll find that they have changed for the better. Even if you have no intention of taking one into the field with you, we urge you to scan a few specimens.

We urge you to read Chapter Nine carefully and to conduct bench tests to familiarize yourself with various samples of which you already know the mineral/metallic content. Such testing will aid you greatly when you encounter samples in the field about whose content you are curious. With your detector you can quickly test all likely samples. You may produce a valuable specimen that has been passed over for years by fellow rockhounds who used their eyes and the other senses but did not possess the electronic "magic" of a modern metal detector.

Thorough and precise bench testing with written notes on the results is vital to the success of a metal detector in the hands of a rockhound. It is important that all of your bench tests be conducted by moving the specimen *across* your searchcoil and that this same method of testing be used with samples in the field. You can then compare your field results with notes that you have made while bench testing.

No matter how proficient you have become as a rockhound, please don't dismiss the potential of a modern metal detector to enhance your capabilities. You may be missing out on real profit opportunities. At a major gem show, Roy encountered an individual selling samples from a famous gold mine and tested some of the samples with a metal detector. Sure enough, they responded as metal.

He pointed this out to the individual selling the samples and hinted that at $3 each some of them might be undervalued. When Roy's suggestion was greeted with scorn, he promptly purchased those samples his detector identified as metal — for $3 each. He later had them sawed into slabs which were purchased by a jewelry maker, some for as high as $125.

If you're a rockhound, the modern metal detector can be a valuable tool. Don't overlook it!

Chapter 14

In Closing
The Law, Health, Safety...

n any primer on finding gold with a metal detector, it is appropriate to consider all aspects of the hobby. In addition to the legal implications of gold hunting, the important matters of health and safety must be taken into account. Some aspects of this subject have already been mentioned; this chapter will review the remainder of our concerns that can affect health and safety. First, however, let's talk about the laws that might pertain to your search for gold.

In the days of the 19th-century gold rushes most of the affected land was public domain which was loosely controlled by the General Land Office and literally "free for the taking" by any U.S. citizen. In fact, such "taking" was encouraged in the Western territories to help settle them.

Of course, most of the early prospectors showed little interest in "settling." Once the current gold strike had played out, they were off to the next bonanza. This condition of free and available land existed in some Western states into the 20th century, but such is no longer the case anywhere. The fact is that *all* land in the United States today is *owned* by some individual or governmental body. Prospecting, as our friend Steve Voynick puts it so clearly in his excellent *Colorado Rockhounding*, "is an activity that may be controlled, restricted or prohibited, depending upon personal policies of private land-owners or, on public lands, upon municipal, state or federal regulations."

The federal government still owns vast territories in most of the major Western gold-producing states. This land is administered by the U. S. Forest Service and the Bureau of Land Management These vast tracts of land offer almost limitless prospecting opportunities. Make certain, however, that you are aware of rules and regulations before you begin trying to find gold on federal land or anywhere else.

It's a good idea to have a general idea of the regulations applicable to treasure hunting, no matter where you are. Each state and many municipalities have such laws that concern where you can hunt and whether you can keep what you find. Make yourself aware of the rules under which you should be operating, no matter where you hunt.

Anywhere you find yourself, however, you will encounter a law against trespassing. All states and cities have such laws. If a sign says, "Keep Out," do just that. It is always best to seek permission, and you may be surprised at how easy it is to obtain when you explain fully just what you're trying to do.

Health ⚬ Safety

It would also be well to mention briefly our concerns for your health and safety. Hunting for gold can be a most pleasant activity. Don't jeopardize it by risking your well-being in any way. We've talked about the potential dangers at old mines, and you may encounter other hazards from time to time. Generally speaking, these will simply be those that confront any picnicker or hiker. Of course, if you're in the wrong place at the right time, there's always the chance of encountering trouble.

Actually, from the standpoint of health and safety the worst things that will usually befall the metal detector hobbyist are sunburn and getting wet or cold in a sudden storm. These dangers, of course, can be minimized by

118

using sunscreen, wearing proper clothing and following common sense rules of exposure.

The hobbyist out hunting for gold with a metal detector, however, can encounter additional difficulties resulting from weather and topography. If you're out in the desert, you face additional dangers from the sun. We urge you never to underestimate the potential dangers of low-humidity desert heat. It can really sneak up on you. Avoid the worst part of the day as much as possible by starting early in the morning. And, protect yourself with the proper coverings for your head and neck as well as sunscreen. You'll want to dress appropriately for the outdoor areas in which you're hunting. That means sturdy shoes or boots and long sleeves and trousers around cactus or spiny plants.

Be especially careful if you're in an unfamiliar area. The experts always say that wild animals and snakes are more afraid of us than we are of them, but pay attention to your surroundings nonetheless. You wouldn't want to step on a rattlesnake sunning itself or go into a cave where a bear is hibernating. The same goes for spiders, scorpions and insects whose bites are painful. Now, all of this may sound pretty outrageous, and we hope you never experience any of it. But, we urge you to be careful. You're out there to find gold and have fun...not to prove anything.

Being careful also entails knowing where you are at all times. That may sound pretty simple while you're scanning in the park back home. When you've crossed a ridge or two avidly seeking (and, finding!) nuggets, and time has simply gotten away from you...learning how quickly twilight falls in the desert mountains can come as an unpleasant surprise. So, we repeat: always know where you are and plan to end your day with plenty of time and daylight to return to your car or camp. You might want to consider searching in a circular pattern that will return you at the end of your day to where you started.

Finally, comes the best rule of all to follow: Use your common sense. That goes not only for your health and safety but for detecting and searching for gold generally. Read this book carefully and learn as much about your detector as possible. Then, use your intelligence to let it help you find gold.

This book has truly been a labor of love for both of us...just as it was when we first wrote such a similar book more than a decade ago. And, now the book has been totally rewritten to incorporate developments in metal detectors that will take us into the 21st Century. Of course, we don't know about you, but it's very difficult for us to realize that this new century is scarcely five years away as this is being written.

Charles' lifetime love, of course, has been for electronic metal detecting generally and for prospecting in particular. Roy shares these feelings. Yet, simply the joy of being alive in the beautiful outdoors of gold country offers pleasure enough for both of us. To have the prospect of adding material wealth doing something that brings such pleasure is, we believe, as close to paradise as one can get on earth.

Rewriting this book began, of course, with long, hard hours spent at work benches in the Garrett Laboratories where the new detectors were developed. Our next labor was taking the new detectors into the gold fields of Arizona, Idaho and Washington where they were field-tested, retested and evaluated. Of course, these are "labors" that we really enjoy! Throughout his career as a manufacturer, Charles has never offered a product to customers until he has tested it thoroughly himself. And, Roy generally participated in this testing, especially where gold-hunting detectors were concerned.

We proved to ourselves many times just how valuable such testing can be. And, because of our experience with each Garrett detector, we can speak knowledgeably about that particular product. We know to what extent it will be of value to the prospector and recreational miner.

Without a doubt the *quality* of a detector taken into the gold fields will have a significant effect on whether gold is found or not. This quality can mean the difference between a pleasant weekend getting exercise outdoors, or doing *exactly the same thing* at a personal profit of, perhaps, hundreds of dollars.

Charles mother used to tell him so often that, "Practice makes perfect." Well, she was close, and he certainly appreciates this training that she gave him. But, it's the continued effort and *correct* practice that makes perfect! Of course, it's impossible to practice correctly without using the right detector and trying to use it properly.

So, read this book thoroughly. Then, make certain that you have the right kind of detector and have spent enough time learning how to use it properly. Patience, too, means more than practice time with your detector. It means being patient with yourself and your surroundings and hunting for hour after hour after hour...even when you don't find anything. Let your watchword be: persevere.

We urge you to be honest with yourself here. The basic ingredients of success in finding gold with a metal detector are the operator's ability to use a versatile and modern ground-balancing instrument correctly and his or her willingness to spend long hours using it. Unless you're working hard with the proper detector, you're limiting yourself and should not expect great success.

Get A Pan

Finally, if you don't have a gold pan, get one. You'll need a plastic pan to help you follow the instructions in this book and you should learn how to pan with it. You'll be surprised at both how easy it is to pan for placer gold and how proud you'll be when you recover a little color from your own pan. Then, once you get the hang of it, you'll find out how much real fun panning can be.

We sincerely hope that you *will* have fun and enjoy hunting for gold with a metal detector. The future for this phase of the hobby is extremely promising. New detectors have opened doors of opportunity as rich discoveries are being made in fields that were explored long ago with older, inferior instruments. Those of us who take advantage of these new opportunities are certain to profit from them.

If you study this book and others, search out the right gold fields and make a determined effort to apply in the field what you learned from your reading, you cannot help but be successful. Remember, too, that while it may be easy to find gold, it's hard to make a living at it. We suggest that you set your sights then on recreation ahead of profit. Make certain that you enjoy yourself! If you get rich, so much the better.

Yet it remains our fondest wish that you are able to fill your poke many times with the earth's treasures. And, we also hope to...

See you in the field!

Appendix 1

Glossary
What Those Words Mean...

rospecting for gold has a terminology that is all its own, stemming from the heritage of the 49'ers and the Klondike. Principal terms used in this book are described, along with others that are related to searching with a metal detector and panning for gold.

All Metal Mode — Another name for the *Deepseeking Mode* of detector operation in which *all* metal targets are detected and the *Searchcoil* can be hovered motionlessly over a target.

Alluvial Gold — Relates to gold that has been deposited by running water, usually in association with silt, sand, gravel or similar material; generally found at considerable distance from the originating *Lode*.

Assay — The evaluation or analysis of *Ore* to determine its metallic content. Usually done chemically with quite accurate results produced.

Automatic Ground Balancing — Circuitry featured on most modern discriminating *Metal Detectors*, requiring no manual adjustments to cancel out detrimental effects of iron earth and salt mineralization. Gold *Nuggets* can sometimes be hunted successfully with *Discriminating Detectors* that include this feature. Some detectors in their *Deepseeking* all metal mode also offer this feature. (See *Ground Track*.)

Avoirdupois Weight — Common American system of weight measure. This system is not used for gold and other precious metals:

1 avoirdupois ounce ....28.350 grams
1 avoirdupois ounce ....437 1/2 grains
16 avoirdupois ounces.............1 avoirdupois pound
16 avoirdupois ounces.............7000 grains

Bedrock — Strata of solid rock underlying unconsolidated surface materials.

Bench Test — Static assessment of capabilities of a *Metal Detector*, usually lying on a bench, table or other surface.

BFO Detector — A type of *Metal Detector* utilizing Beat Frequency Oscillator (BFO) circuitry. In the 1960s and 1970s these were the *Metal Detectors* best suited to hunt for gold. The instruments are important in the evolution of *Metal Detector* development. Although some older hobbyists continue to use such models, they are difficult to operate, produce less than satisfactory results and are, thus, obsolete. BFO detectors are now considered totally unsuitable for finding gold when compared with the capabilities of modern instruments.

Black Sand — *See Magnetic Black Sand.*

Claim — A tract of land that has been legally staked out and filed with the proper governmental agency to afford exclusive prospecting purposes for gold and/or other metals.

Classifier — Device designed to fit atop a *Gold Pan* through which materials going into the pan are passed. The classifier is made of plastic, metal or some other ma-

Seeking tiny gold nuggets Charles Garrett uses a modern detector in its Deepseeking all metal mode, continually ground balanced by Ground Track.

terial and is designed to eliminate rocks and other large pieces from the *Gold Pan* itself. Also called a *Grizzly*.

Color — A term used for minute specks of gold in gravel. Often used colloquially to describe any traces of gold found by *Panning*.

Computerized Detector — A *Metal Detector* whose circuitry contains an integrated circuit containing the necessary elements of a small digital computer. This *Microprocessor* chip gives the detector "memory" that enables it to perform automatically numerous functions that are the responsibility of the operator of a detector without such a microprocessor, if the functions are indeed ever performed at all.

Concentrates — Heavier materials (gold, black sand, etc.) that remain after proper *Panning* of sand/rocks/gravel.

Deepseeking Mode — Mode of detector operation in which *all* metal targets are detected. Precise *Ground Balancing*, either automatic or manual, is essential in this mode to eliminate or minimize the effects of mineralization in the soil. This mode of detector operation should be used for most effective gold hunting, particularly in seeking gold flakes or *Nuggets* that may be very small or deeply buried. In this mode the *Searchcoil* can be hovered motionlessly over a target.

Discriminate Mode — The mode of operation of a *Metal Detector* in which certain metallic targets are specifically designated by the operator to be eliminated from detection. It is the mode of operation offered by a *Discriminating Detector*, and is a secondary mode offered

Authors of this book have proved countless times that gold in all its forms can be found when modern metal detectors are used properly and patiently.

by some gold-hunting detectors with a *Deepseeking Mode*. It is used on such detectors for the testing and elimination of *Hot Rocks*. Because they offer this mode, deepseeking, gold-hunting detectors can search effectively for coins, jewelry and all other items.

Discriminating Detector — One of today's most popular type of instruments, especially for hunting coins and searching beaches. Featuring *Automatic Ground Balance*, this type of instrument was initially referred to as a Motion Detector since it can respond to a target only while the *Searchcoil* is being moved over that target.

Discrimination — The ability of specific circuits within a detector to eliminate from detection certain undesirable metallic objects. On any detector to be used in hunting for gold, it is important that the *Zero Discrimination Point* be precisely adjusted at the factory for metal vs. mineral identification.

Dredge — See *Suction Dredge*.

Dry Panning — Panning for gold with no liquid available to create the state of fluid *Suspension* in which gravity sinks gold flakes into the *Riffles* of a *Gravity Trap Gold Pan*. Dry panning achieves similar results by persistently working to eliminate the larger pieces of material while allowing gold to settle into the *Riffles*.

Dry Washer — A type of mechanical device designed to utilize gravity for separating gold from other materials when water is not available.

Dust — Particles of gold so minute they resemble dust. In the gold rush days the amount of dust a miner (or, bartender) could pinch between his thumb and forefinger was considered $1.

Electronic Prospecting — Using a *Metal Detector* to search for gold, silver or other precious metals. Most common prospecting is the search for gold *Nuggets*.

Elliptical Searchcoil — Oval-shaped *Searchcoil* with length approximately twice its width. Intended initially for use by hobbyists hunting for gold in tight, rocky spaces, the design has now been enhanced to provide deep, "knife-edge" scanning, and these coils are used in all types of treasure hunting.

Fast Track™ — A type of detector circuitry with computerized microprocessor controls, that automatically *Ground Balances* a detector's *Deepseeking* circuitry.

Float — Chunk of ore broken off from the *Lode* and moved (usually down hill) by gravity, wind, water, earth movement or some other act of nature.

Flour Gold — Extremely fine-grain *Placer* gold that is almost the consistency of flour.

Ferrous — Pertains to iron and iron compounds, such as nails or bottlecaps.

Fool's Gold — See *Pyrite*.

Free Milling — Method of processing *Ore* designed to reduce it to gold or other desired metal without use of heat, chemicals or other processes. Areas that used such processes are considered ideal for metal detecting.

Gold Pan — A broad, shallow and open container in which materials suspected of containing gold can be placed in a liquid *Suspension* that allows gold to sink to the bottom because it is heavier than the other substances. Pans are usually made of metal or plastic.

Gold Panning Kit — A compact kit offered by Garrett that includes 14-inch and 10 1/2-inch *Gravity Trap* pans, a classifier and a suction bottle for vacuuming up microscopic gold, plus an illustrated instruction booklet.

Graphic Target Analyzer™ — Device on a *Metal Detector* that reports continuously and visually on an LCD such information as depth and type of target, audio and tone levels, sensitivity, battery condition, etc.

Gravity Trap™ Gold Pan — The patented (U.S. Patent #4,162,969) *Gold Pan* featuring 90° *Riffles* made and sold by Garrett. Its forest green color and plastic composition have been field-tested and proven to be the most effective of all colors and materials.

Grizzly — See *Classifier*.

Ground Balancing — The process of adjusting a *Metal Detector*'s circuitry, either manually or automatically, to eliminate (ignore or cancel) the detection effect of iron minerals or wetted salt. Such adjustment is vital in seeking gold, especially flakes or tiny nuggets.

Ground Canceling — See *Ground Balancing.*

Ground Track™ — Microprocessor-controlled detector circuitry that automatically *Ground Balances* a detector's *Deepseeking* (all metal) circuitry and continually maintains proper *Ground Balance* while the detector is being scanned.

Hardrock Mining — The sinking of a main shaft with additional shafts or drifts then cut to follow veins of gold from the main deposit. Conducted properly, this type of mining requires a sizable investment.

Headphones — *Metal Detector* accessory that converts electrical energy waves into audible waves of identical form. Used in place of detector loudspeakers, especially in noisy or windy locations. Because they present the audible signals more effectively than a loudspeaker, headphones are especially recommended for use in gold hunting. They will permit hearing the faint signals from tiny or deeply buried *Nuggets.*

High Grade Specimen — *Nugget* or ore sample with large percentage of gold or other conductive mineral.

Hip Mount — A detector configuration once popular because of the heavy control housings on older detectors. While this configuration is built into the Garrett's GTA detectors (belt- mounted battery pack) and is an option on the Scorpion Gold Stinger, most gold hunters do not consider it important because of the light weight of the Stinger and other modern instruments.

Hot Rock — Mineralized rock that is "misplaced" geologically and produces a positive signal. Mineral content of the rock is, thus, different from its environment for which the detector has been *Ground Balanced.* Distinguishing hot rocks is easily accomplished with a properly calibrated detector in its *Discriminate Mode.*

Hydraulic Mining — Recovery of gold through the discharge of water under great pressure against a deposit.

The water's force flushes the silt and gravel through *Sluices* where it can be separated and the gold recovered.

Karat — Unit of fineness for gold. Pure gold is 24 karats. When used in jewelry, gold is often strengthened by the addition of other metals, and the alloy is thus identified as 18k (75% gold), 12k (50% gold), etc.

Leaching — A gold production technique in which chemicals and other liquids are used to free gold from the rock that surrounds it.

Lode — Metallic vein in the earth's crust, especially gold or silver, and the source of *Placer* gold.

Magnetic Black Sand — Magnetite, a magnetic oxide of iron and, sometimes, hematite; may also contain titanium and other rare-earth minerals but serves mainly as an indicator of the possible presence of *Placer* gold.

Manual Ground Balance — *Metal Detector* circuit that permits precise canceling (ignoring or eliminating) the detrimental effects of iron earth and salt mineralization. Not included on *Discriminating Detectors.*

Metal Detector — Electronic instrument or device, usually battery-powered, capable of sensing the presence of conductive metallic objects, such as gold *Nuggets;* then, providing its operator with an audible and/or visual indication of that object's location.

Metal/Mineral — Refers primarily to the *Zero Discrimination* point important in eliminating *Hot Rocks.* On a properly calibrated detector signals at this zero point will indicate whether a target is metal or mineral.

Microprocessor — An integrated circuit containing the necessary elements of a small digital computer. When used in a modern *Metal Detector* the "memory" of a microprocessor enables the detector to perform automatically numerous functions that can remarkably enhance its capabilities.

Mode — The manner in which a detector operates, usually controlled by the operator. Modern universal detectors generally offer two modes, *Deepseeking* (all metal) and *Discriminate.*

Non-Ferrous — Pertains to non-iron metals/compounds, such as brass, silver, gold, lead, aluminum, etc.

Notch Discrimination — Form of *Discrimination* on Garrett's GTA detectors that permits levels of conductivity to be eliminated from detection simultaneously.

Nugget — A lump of precious metal found in nature. Gold nuggets can range in size from tiny pinhead-size flecks to huge "rocks" that weigh several pounds.

Null — A tuning or audio adjustment condition that results in "quiet" or zero audio operation.

Ore — Source material which is mined or worked for the extraction of precious metals.

Panning — See *Gold Pan*.

Pinpointing — The ability of a detector operator to determine exactly where a detected target is located. On modern detectors this function is performed automatically when the Pinpoint mode is activated.

Placer — Pronounced like "plaster" without the "t," the term describes an accumulation of gold, black magnetic sand and other elements whose specific gravity is higher than the sand, rock, etc. with which it is found; generally gold-bearing gravel.

Pyrite — Used to identify many compounds of metals resembling gold, usually with sulfur or arsenic, especially iron pyrites or copper pyrites. Pyrite is brass-yellow and brittle, but because of its color is often mistaken for gold and identified as "fool's gold."

Quartz — Commonly found in association with gold *Lodes* or veins, consists of pure silica or silicon dioxide. Most gold taken from the earth by *Hardrock Mining* comes from quartz veins.

Riffles — The 90° grooves on the lower side of a *Gravity Trap Gold Pan* and *Super Sluice* into which forces of gravity cause gold to sink and be effectively separated from other materials. Riffles enable gold to be panned (wet or dry) more thoroughly and rapidly.

Scanning — The actual movement of a *Searchcoil* over the ground or other area being searched.

Searchcoil — Component of a *Metal Detector* that houses its transmitter and receiver antennas. Usually attached to the control housing by an adjustable stem, the *Searchcoil* is scanned over the ground or other area being searched.

Signal — Generally describes the electromagnetic data received by a *Metal Detector* from a target and the audio and/or visual response generated by it.

Silent Audio — The tuning of the audio level of a detector in the "silent" (just below *Threshold*) zone. When operating in this fashion, the operator hears no sound at all until a target is detected. This method is *not* recommended in hunting for gold because slight variations in sound, so important in locating tiny or deeply buried *Nuggets*, might be overlooked.

Sluice — Device through which water is induced to flow; contains "slots" into which gravity sinks gold and other heavier materials, permitting them to be separated; sometimes called "sluice box" because of its usual box-like appearance.

Sniping — Testing of a location by selective use of the *Gold Pan*, alone or in combination with *Metal Detector*, *Dredge* or other tools.

Suction Dredge — Floating device with motor and tubing to recover material from lake/stream bottoms, plus *Sluice* box for gravity separation of precious metals.

Super Sluice — New Garrett gold recovery device with *Gravity Trap Riffles* a full one-half inch deep. So named because it is virtually a hand-held *Sluice*.

Super Sniper™ — A Garrett trademark used to describe its 4 1/2-inch *Searchcoil* and the method (Super sniping) for using it to enhance individual target detection in specialized situations. In hunting for gold the small coil can be especially effective in areas with large amounts of metal "junk" or near metallic objects such as fences, posts, buildings, etc. Outstanding for detection of tiny, pinhead-size nuggets and for locating placer concentrations in wet or dry situations.

Suspension — Status of a substance when its particles are mixed with, but undissolved in, fluid. In this state of suspension gravity will cause flakes of gold to sink into *Riffles* of a gold pan or sluice.

Tailings — Refuse that remains after precious metal has been recovered, usually by mining or dredging.

Threshold — Adjustable level of audio sound at which a *Metal Detector* is operated when searching for gold. It is recommended that a very low, but audible, level of sound be maintained.

TR Disc — A mode of *Metal Detector* operation that was important in evolution of the instrument. In this mode *Discrimination* could be achieved with *Manual Ground Balance*. Most modern detectors do not offer this mode since it is not required on an instrument with precise *Zero Discrimination*.

Trommel — The screening device on a dredge; used to size rocks or ore.

Troy Ounce — Slightly heavier than an avoirdupois ounce. The Troy weight system is used for measurement of gold and other precious metals:

1 troy ounce ....31.103 grams
24 grains...................1 pennyweight
20 pennyweights ....1 troy ounce
480 grains...................1 troy ounce
12 ounces...................1 troy pound

Wet Panning — The act of panning for gold with liquid (usually water) being used to create the state of *Suspension* that makes it easier for gravity to cause gold flakes to sink into the *Riffles* of a *Gravity Trap Gold Pan* or *Super Sluice*.

Zero Discrimination — That point in the circuitry of a detector when it provides no discrimination and detects all metal objects. On gold-hunting detectors this point must be precisely set at the factory for metal vs. mineral identification. On GTA detectors this point is achieved when any *Notch Discrimination* is eliminated by making certain that all segments on the Lower Scale are visible.

Appendix 2

SOURCES
Can Help You Find Gold

B asic sources for information on areas where gold might be found are given in this section. Many of these offices provide packets containing considerable information about the area and the potential for finding gold there.

Because the agency is concerned with recreational use of land, the Bureau of Land Management can usually be particularly helpful. All addresses were current in the autumn of 1995.

Bureau of Land Management
U. S. Department of the Interior

The Bureau of Land Management, an agency within the Department of the Interior, is responsible for managing 272 million acres of public lands and resources...about one-eighth of our nation's land area. The terrain, consisting of mountains, prairie and tundra, is located primarily in the Western states where gold-producing regions can be found All BLM State Offices are listed below, together with cities and towns in which BLM District, Resource, Area and other offices are located.

Alaska State Office
222 W. 7th Ave. #13
Anchorage, AK 99513-7599
Other BLM offices in Fairbanks, Ft. Wainwright, Glennallen, Nome and Tok.

Arizona State Office
P. O. Box 16563
Phoenix, AZ 85011-6553
Other Arizona BLM offices in Kingman, Lake Havasu City, Huachuca City, Stafford, Yuma and St. George

California State Office
2800 Cottage Way E-2841
Sacramento, CA 95825-1889
Other BLM offices in Alturas, Arcata, Bakersfield, Barstow, Bishop, Cedarville, El Centro, Folsom, Hollister, Needles, Palm Springs, Redding, Ridgecrest, Riverside, Susanville and Ukiah.

Colorado State Office
2850 Youngfield St.
Lakewood, CO 80215
Other BLM offices in Alamosa, Canon City, Craig, Denver, Dolores, Durango, Glenwood Springs, Grand Junction, Gunnnison, Kremming, Meeker and Montrose.

Idaho State Office
3380 Americana Terrace
Boise, ID 83706
Other BLM offices in Boise, Burley, Coeur d'Alene, Cottonwood, Idaho Falls, Malad, Pocatello, Salmon and Shoshone.

Montana State Office
P. O. Box 368000
Billings, MT 59107
Other Montana BLM offices in Billings, Butte, Dillon, Ekalaka, Lewistown, Glasgow, Great Falls, Havre, Malta, Miles City, Missoula, Belle Fourche, SD, and Dickinson, ND.

Nevada State Office
P. O. Box 12000
Reno, NV 89520
Other BLM offices in Battle Mountain, Carson City, Caliente, Elko, Ely, Las Vegas, Sparks, Tonopah and Winnemucca.

New Mexico State Office
P. O. Box 27115
Santa Fe, NM 87502-0015
Other BLM offices in Albuquerque, Carlsbad, Farmington, Grant, Hobbs, Las Cruces, Roswell, Socorro and Taos and Moore and Tulsa, OK.

Oregon State Office
P. O. Box 2965
Portland, OR 97208
Other BLM offices in Baker, Coos Bay, Eugene, Klamath Falls, Lakeview, Medford, Hines, Prineville, Roseburg, Salem, Tillamook, Vale and Spokane and Wentachee, WA.

Utah State Office
324 State St. Suite 301
Salt Lake City UT 84111-2303
Other BLM offices in Cedar City, Escalante, Fillmore, Grouse Creek, Hanksville, Kanab, Moab, Monticello, Price, Richfield, St. George and Vernal.

Wyoming State Office
P. O. Box 1828
Cheyenne, WY 82003
Other BLM offices in Buffalo, Casper, Cody, Kemmerer, Lander, Mills, Newcastle, Pinedale, Rawlins, Rock Springs and Worland.

Eastern States Office 7450 Boston Blvd.
Springfield, VA 22153
Other Eastern States BLM offices in Jackson, MS; Rolla, MO; and Milwaukee, WI.

BLM Service Center
Denver Federal Center
P. O. Box 25047
Denver, CO 80255

BLM Headquarters
Department of the Interior
18th and C Streets N.W.
Washington, D.C. 20240

Forest Service Regions
U. S. Department of Agriculture

Alaska Region
Federal Office Bldg.
P. O. Box 21628
Juneau, AK 99802-1628

Intermountain Region
324 25th St.
Ogden, UT 84401

Northern Region
P. O. Box 7669
Missoula, MT 59807

Pacific Southwest Region
630 Sansome Street
San Francisco, CA 94111

Rocky Mountain Region
740 Simms St.
Lakewood, CO 80225

Southwestern Region
517 Gold Ave. SW
Albuquerque, NM 87102

Pacific Northwest Region
P. O. Box 3623
Portland, OR 97208-3623

State Bureaus

Alaska Dept. of
Natural Resources
3700 Airport Way
Fairbanks, AK 99709

Arizona Geol. Survey
416 W. Congress St. #100
Tucson, AZ 85701

California Div. of Mines
and Geology
P. O. Box 2980
Sacramento, CA 95812

Colorado Tourism Bd.
1625 Broadway #1700
Denver, CO 80202

Idaho Geol. Survey
Morrill Hall, Room 332
University of Idaho
Moscow, ID 83844-3014

Montana Bur. of Mines
Montana Tech of the
University of Montana
1300 West Park Street
Butte, MT 59701-8997

New Mexico Bur. of Mines
& Mineral Recources
Campus Station
Socorro, NM 87801

Oregon Dept. of Geology
800 NE Oregon Street #28
Portland, OR 97232

South Dakota Geological
Survey
Akeley Science Center
University of South Dakota
414 East Clark St.
Vermillion, SD 57069-2390

Utah Geological Survey
2623 S. Foothill Drive
Salt Lake City, UT 84109

Washington Department
of Natural Resources
Div. of Geology & Earth
P. O. Box 47007
Olympia, WA 98504-7007

Wyoming Geol. Survey
P. O. Box 3008 Univ. Sta.
Laramie, WY 82071

Nevada Bureau of Mines & Geology/178
Publications Office, 310 Sem Bldg
University of Nevado, Reno
Reno, NV 89557-0088

RAM Books
Order Form

Please send me the following RAM Books:

- ☐ New Successful Coin Hunting...............................$9.95
- ☐ Treasure Hunting for Fun and Profit.......................$9.95
- ☐ Ghost Town Treasures..$9.95
- ☐ Find Gold with a Metal Detector..............................$9.95
- ☐ Buried Treasures You Can Find.............................$14.95
- ☐ Gold of the Americas..$9.95
- ☐ Treasure Recovery From Sand and Sea.................$7.95
- ☐ New Modern Metal Detectors...............................$12.95
- ☐ Gold Panning is Easy..$9.95
- ☐ Introduction to Metal Detecting*.............................$1.00
- ☐ Competitive Treasure Hunting.................................$9.95
- ☐ Find an Ounce of Gold a Day..................................$3.00
- ☐ Treasure Caches Can be Found.............................$9.95

Add $1.00 for each book. (Maximum of $3.00) for shipping and handling.
*No $1.00 shipping charge when ordered with another book.

Send order form and payment to:
Garrett Metal Detectors
RAM Publishing
1881 West State Street
Garland, Texas 75042

Total book purchase amount.............$ _____

8.25% tax (Texas & California residents only).. .$ _____

Shipping and Handling......................$ _____

Total...$ _____

Please check one
☐   Enclosed is my check or money order
☐   I prefer to pay using my credit card (check one)
         ☐ American Express   ☐ MasterCard
         ☐ Visa   ☐ Discover

Please fill out the following information:

_____
Credit Card Number (include expiration date)

_____
Name

_____
Shipping Address

_____
City, State, Zip Code

_____
Signature (all credit card orders must be signed)